PhotoPlus X4
Resource Guide

How to contact us

Web:

Serif Website: http://www.serif.com

Forums: http://www.serif.com/forums.asp

Main office (UK, Europe):

The Software Centre, PO Box 2000, Nottingham, NG11 7GW, UK

Main: (0115) 914 2000

Registration (UK only):   (0800) 376 1989

Sales (UK only):   (0800) 376 7070

Customer Service/
Technical Support: http://www.support.serif.com/

General Fax: (0115) 914 2020

North American office (US, Canada):

Serif Inc, The Software Center, 17 Hampshire Drive, Suite 1 & 2, Hudson, NH 03051, USA

Main: (603) 889-8650

Registration: (800) 794-6876

Sales: (800) 489 6703

Customer Service/
Technical Support: http://www.support.serif.com/

General Fax: (603) 889-1127

International:

Please contact your local distributor/dealer. For further details, please contact us at one of our phone numbers above.

Introduction

Welcome to the PhotoPlus X4 Resource Guide!

Whether you are new to PhotoPlus or a seasoned professional, the Resource Guide offers content to help you get the best out of PhotoPlus.

Offering a range of beginner-level and advanced tutorials, along with full-colour previews of the PhotoPlus macros and brushes, we hope you'll find this Resource Guide to be a valuable resource that you'll return to time and time again.

The Resource Guide is organized into the following chapters:

1: Tutorials

Provides introductory exercises to help new users master the basics, and more challenging projects for experienced users.

2: Makeover Studio

Includes professional retouching effects such as teeth whitening, skin smoothing, dark circle reduction, and more.

3: Macros

Showcases the extensive selection of predefined macros, available from the **Macros** tab, that let you quickly enhance, manipulate, and apply creative effects to your images.

4: Brushes

Provides a visual reference guide to the PhotoPlus brush tips and picture brushes, and explains how to use them.

5: PhotoFix Presets

New to PhotoPlus X4, **PhotoFix** provides an environment that simplifies the often complicated process of image correction. This chapter showcases the preset filters provided on the **Favourites** tab.

Contents

Introduction

Chapter 5 - PhotoFix Presets 283

Tutorials

These PhotoPlus tutorials provide illustrated, step-by-step instructions to show you how to get from the initial image to the end result.

You can apply these techniques to your own photographs, or use the samples available online (see individual tutorials for details).

This chapter is divided into two sections:

- **Adjusting Photographs** (p. 5): Guiding you through various ways of improving and rescuing photos.

- **Creative Effects** (p. 89): Giving you inspiration for transforming your photos into art.

Accessing the tutorials

You can access the tutorials in one of the following ways:

- From the PhotoPlus Startup Wizard, select from the **Learning** section. Different icons indicate the type of tutorial available.

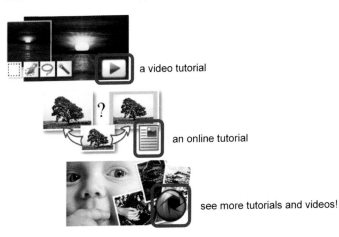

a video tutorial

an online tutorial

see more tutorials and videos!

- or -

- From PhotoPlus, click **Help** and then click **Tutorials**.

Accessing the sample files

Throughout the tutorials, you'll be prompted to access sample files. All samples are accessible via the Internet at the following location:

http://go.serif.com/resources/HPX4

If you've clicked on a file, you can either open or save the file. We recommend you save the file to your desktop or a named folder on your computer.

Adjusting Photographs

Whether you're a novice, amateur, or professional photographer, there will always be some photos that need some type of modification. Some will only need a minor tweak to get them looking fantastic while others, perhaps old or damaged, might require substantial work. Whatever is needed, we'll show you the steps to take to get that picture looking perfect.

Key Adjustments

Learn about the various methods you can use to sharpen and enhance a photograph.

By the end of this tutorial you will be able to:

- Make **Levels** and **Curves** adjustments

- Use an **Unsharp Mask** filter

- Use the **Sharpen Tool**

For this tutorial, you can either use your own photos or follow along exactly by using ours.

Go to **http://go.serif.com/resources/HPX4** to download the following tutorial project file(s):

⊙ **cat.jpg**

Let's begin...

- On the Standard toolbar, click 📂 **Open**.

- Locate **cat.jpg** (or your own photo) and click **Open**.

  The image opens in the workspace.

Our image isn't bad overall but lacks contrast and looks a little flat. We'll begin by making an easy adjustment and then move on to the professional favourites later in the tutorial.

> 🖋 Although all the image adjustments made in this exercise can be applied directly to an image, for best practice we'll be using adjustment layers and filter layers.
>
> Adjustment layers and filter layers provide more flexibility and let you apply changes experimentally without affecting your original image. You can turn these layers on and off to compare 'before' and 'after' images, and can easily edit and delete them later.

Levels

The **Levels** dialog displays the proportion of image pixels at each lightness value, ranging from shadows through to highlights. By looking at the histogram, you can see if the image lacks a 'high end' or a 'low end,' and adjust the **black** or **white** point accordingly.

To apply a levels adjustment:

1   On the **Adjustments** tab, click **Levels...**

A new adjustment layer is added.

2   The histogram on the **Adjustments** tab shows that the image is lacking a low end. Correct this by dragging the black point slider to the edge of the histogram (around input level 38).

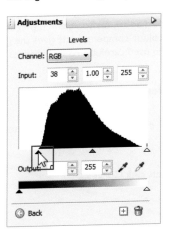

Immediately the image has more contrast and the pattern of the fur is more defined.

Now let's see what happens when we adjust the Curves...

Curves

This is probably the professional photographer's favourite adjustment. The **Curves** adjustment lets you correct the tonal range of an image—the spread of lightness values through shadow, midtone, and highlight regions—and control individual colour components. It gives the greatest control of the midtones and when used carefully, really enhances an image.

To apply a curves adjustment:

1   On the **Layers** tab, click the 👁 **Hide/Show Layer** button for the **Levels** adjustment layer.

2   On the **Adjustments** tab, click **Curves...**

3   The **Adjustments** tab shows the **Curves** graph:

- Click and drag the lower half of the line down to increase the shadows.

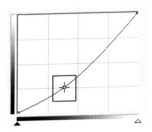

- Click and drag the upper half of the line up to boost the highlights.

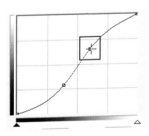

- Adjust the line on the graph until you are happy with the results.

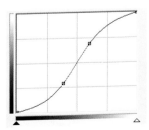

For best effect, you should aim for a gentle S-shape.

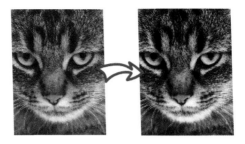

You'll see that the image looks much brighter and displays great contrast. The curves adjustment has almost caused the colours to "pop" out of the page.

This is probably the most difficult adjustment to master, but with practice, it produces some great results. It also works equally well with greyscale images.

> Sometimes you'll need to boost midtones to correct a poor exposure. To do this, push the centre of the curve upwards. Take care when doing this as the results can often look unnatural if the curve is pushed too far.

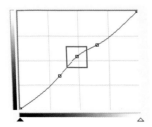

Unsharp Mask

Unsharp Mask works mainly to enhance the edges in an image. It is generally considered to be the standard tool for adjusting sharpness in photographs. It is excellent for improving image quality, especially with scanned or resized pictures. You can apply this correction on a **filter layer** (recommended), or directly to your image.

Unsharp Mask is a filter effect so we'll apply it as a **filter layer**.

To apply an Unsharp Mask:

1   On the **Layers** tab, click the ☜ **Hide/Show Layer** button for the **Levels** and **Curves** adjustment layers.

2   Next, right-click on the **Background** layer, click **Duplicate...** and then, in the dialog, rename the layer 'Unsharp Mask'.

3   Finally, right-click on the new layer and click **Convert to Filter Layer**.

4   On the **Effects** menu, click **Sharpen > Unsharp Mask...**

5   In the dialog enter the following values by either typing into the input boxes or by dragging the sliders:

   • **Amount** 20%

   • **Radius** 50.0

   • **Threshold** 0

💡 For fine detail and/or low resolution images, use a lower radius setting (to avoid obliterating detail). Use higher settings with higher resolution images, where pixels are smaller relative to image elements.

🖋 Set the threshold value too high and you'll see very little change in your image. Generally, values between 0 and 5 are useful. Use a higher threshold for grainy images or skin tones (5 or sometimes more), so the filter won't merely amplify noise in the image.

6   Click **OK**. The filter appears beneath the filter layer on the **Layers** tab.

Note especially that the detail around the eyes and whiskers has been brought out, without over-exposing the white fur.

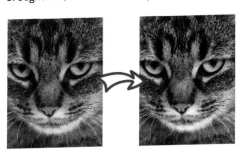

💡 For optimum sharpening of an entire photograph, use the Unsharp Mask filter and experiment with different settings until you achieve the desired results.

💡 When choosing sharpening settings, don't forget to consider your image resolution and output (print or screen). In general, use a higher Radius setting for higher resolution images intended for print, less radius for lower resolution images that will be viewed on screen.

The finishing touch

In this final example we will combine the earlier adjustments to achieve the final result—a great looking image. This also highlights the advantage of using adjustment and filter layers!

• On the **Layers** tab, click the 👁 **Hide/Show Layer** button to show the **Unsharp Mask**, **Levels** and **Curves** layers.

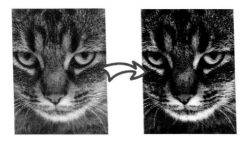

The technique you choose depends on the image you are working on. Other adjustments are covered in the Help and in some of the other tutorials. Experiment with different images (both colour and greyscale) and adjustments and see what works for you. Have fun!

Image or Canvas Size?

In PhotoPlus there are options to change the **image size** and to change the **canvas size**, but what's the difference? How do you know which one to choose? Let's find out...

Image Size

When you change **image size**, you are scaling the whole image (or selected region) up or down.

You will change the image size when:

- enlarging the image for print.

- reducing the image for on-screen display.

- reducing the image to create a thumbnail for a website.

Canvas Size

Changing the canvas size simply involves adding or taking away pixels around the edges of the image. It is like adding to the neutral border around a mounted photo, or using scissors to crop the photo to a smaller size. The image, or part of the image that is left after a crop, is unchanged.

You will change the canvas size when:

• you want to add a border to your image (without changing the size of the image itself).

• you crop an image.

Now that you know the difference between image size and canvas size, why not take a look at the tutorials to see how to change the size of your images!

Cropping I

Every image has boundaries, and you can decide where those boundaries should be. Cropping is an easy, yet often overlooked, step when editing photos. In this tutorial, we'll show you how to use the various tools in PhotoPlus to crop your images to add visual impact and focus. For more on why you should crop images, see **Cropping II** (p. 27).

By the end of this tutorial you will be able to:

- Define a crop selection size using the **Crop Tool**.

- Crop to a pre-defined print size.

- Use the **Thirds Grid** to aid photo composition.

- Crop to a selection.

Let's begin...

- On the Standard toolbar, click 🖱 **Open**.

- Locate a photo (ideally with a definite subject, as this will be easier) and click **Open**.

  The image opens in the workspace.

Cropping an image

When you crop an image, PhotoPlus deletes all of the pixels outside the crop selection area, and resizes the image canvas so that only the area inside the crop selection remains.

⚠ In Windows, always make a copy of the original, rather than use the original image itself. If you work on an original, make a mistake and then save the image, the changes are permanent and cannot be undone. However if you preserve the original, you can start the process again using a duplicate copy.

You can crop larger areas when photos are shot at a high resolution rather than a low one. Keep this in mind before taking photos and make sure your camera is set to its highest resolution and image quality.

To crop the image with Crop Tool:

1   On the Tools toolbar, select the ⬛ **Crop Tool**.

2   Drag out a rectangular crop selection area on the image. (To constrain the region to a square, hold down the **Ctrl** key while dragging.)

     The area that will be deleted turns dark.

3   If required, click and drag inside the selection to move the whole crop area (the cursor changes to the **Move** cursor), or drag the sizing handles.

4   On the Crop context toolbar, click 🔵 to crop to the designated size (or double-click inside the selected area). The crop is applied.

To use the Rule of Thirds grid:

1   On the Tools toolbar, select the ⊠ **Crop Tool**.

2   On the Crop context toolbar:

  •   Select the **Thirds grid** check box.

  •   Choose a pre-defined, Custom, or **Unconstrained** crop
        selection area.

3   Drag to define your crop area. A 3 x 3 grid is superimposed on your
      image (highlighted yellow).

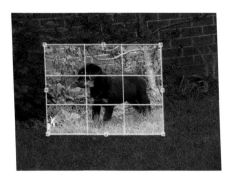

4   For best results, position the subject of the photo at any of the four
    intersection points on the grid.

5   Double-click inside the crop selection (or click 🌑) to crop to the
    outer grid dimensions.

As you can see, a close crop can completely change the focus of an image.
For more information about the Rule of Thirds, see the **Rule of Thirds**
tutorial (p. 35).

To crop to a pre-defined print size:

1   On the Tools toolbar, select the ⬚ **Crop Tool**.

2   On the Crop context toolbar, in the left-most drop-down list, choose
    a pre-defined print size. We chose 7 x 5 in.

3   Drag out to define your crop selection area.

4   Double-click inside the crop selection to crop to the designated size. The print resolution adjusts to honour the print dimensions.

In PhotoPlus you can also crop to selections. This allows you to be more creative with your cropping. Let's look at this now...

To crop to selection:

1   On the Tools toolbar, expand the Selection tools flyout and choose any of the Selection tools. We chose the ☆ **Star Selection Tool**.

2   Drag to define a crop selection area.

3   If required, click and drag inside the selection to reposition the
     selection area. If you have used one of the QuickShape selections,
     position any nodes and double-click in the shape to change it to an
     active selection.

4   **Optional:** On the Tools toolbar, click the ✐ **Colour Pickup
     Tool**. Right-click on an area of the image to select a background
     colour.

5   On the **Image** menu, click **Crop to Selection**.

As you can see, the image is cropped to the star shape and the space
around the shape is filled with the background colour set in step **4**.
Why not combine this with changing the canvas size to give the image
an interesting frame?

Cropping II

In this tutorial we'll illustrate some effective and powerful cropping techniques to improve your images and turn ordinary images into something stylish and dynamic!

By the end of this tutorial you will be able to:

- Reinvent a photo by cropping it to create a landscape or portrait rotation.

- Use cropping as a way to zoom into an important area of a photo.

- Throw away your fears and crop drastically to enhance your photo compositions.

Why crop?

Cropping is easy and, when planned carefully, can greatly improve the composition and visual impact of a digital photo. Here are a few of the main reasons why you should crop an image:

- Improve photo composition.

- Give your image focus.

- "Zoom in" on a subject.

- Change the canvas orientation to better suit the composition.

- Change the aspect ratio for print or web.

- Get creative and add originality and drama.

⚠ In Windows, always make a copy of the original, rather than use the original image itself. If you work on an original, make a mistake and then save the image, the changes are permanent and can not be undone. However if you preserved the original, you can start the process again using a duplicate copy.

💡 You can crop larger areas when photos are shot at a high resolution rather than a low one. Keep this in mind before taking photos and make sure your camera is set to its highest resolution and image quality.

1. Improve composition

One of the best ways of improving composition is to use the Rule of Thirds. We mentioned this rule in **Cropping I** (p. 19), and it even has its own dedicated tutorial (p. 35), but it's so important in photo composition, we've mentioned it here as well. Divide your image into a 3 x 3 grid and position the main focal points along one or more of the intersecting lines.

We've used the rule to further improve the composition of the already great shot of a blue tit.

If you look closely, you'll see that we've obeyed this rule in nearly all of our examples! Just as a reminder, you can add a **Rule of Thirds** grid to any crop selection by selecting the **Thirds grid** check box on the Crop context toolbar. The Rule of Thirds is also a great way to add impact to otherwise normal images. However, as with all rules, sometimes it's good to break them!

When photographing people, it is common to line the body up with a vertical line, and have the subject's eyes in line with a horizontal one.

You should always consider the path of moving subjects and, generally, leave space in front of them into which they can move. You can see this happening in our example from the Isle of Man TT 2010 Superbike race. Notice how it gives the image more movement.

It is also important to remove any part of the photo that doesn't contribute to the overall effect.

2. Give your image focus

Composition and focus often go hand in hand. A good photo should draw the eye to the main subject instantly. If you have a lot of distracting elements in the background of your image, crop them out!

3. Zooming in

Zooming closely into a subject can strengthen a focal point. Extreme cropping can highlight fascinating details. Our close crop of this beach motocross photo highlights the concentration in the eyes of the rider.

4. Change orientation

You may find that a certain orientation suits some photos better than others. If you haven't allowed for this when taking your photo with your camera, change it with a crop!

5. Cropping for print

Many digital cameras will take photos which do not conform to the standard print layouts, 6 x 4, 7 x 5, 10 x 8, etc.

Before taking your digital photos to be processed, or printing them yourself, you can crop your photo to one of the set print ratios so it looks exactly how you want it to look once printed.

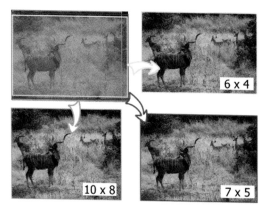

Get creative

Add drama to an otherwise dull photo!

You don't have to stick to traditional photo print sizes. Experiment with different crops...

Wide angle crop of the second sidecar race at the Isle of Man TT 2010:

Square crop from the Isle of Man TT 2010 race, and beside it, the drama of beach racing in Peel, Isle of Man.

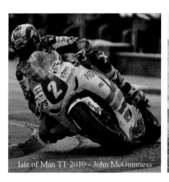 

You could even rotate the image before applying the crop and add movement by changing the position of the horizon!

You could also combine cropping and canvas resizing with other PhotoPlus layer techniques such as layer masking to get a really punchy image (again from the Isle of Man Dainese Senior TT 2010 race).

Now that you know more about cropping techniques, have fun making your own dynamic images!

Master the Rule of Thirds

Have you ever wondered how to get a stronger composition out of your images? Try the Rule of Thirds! In this tutorial you will learn about this rule and how you can use it to highlight the best features in your shots.

In the above images, the second was cropped using the Rule of Thirds. Which do you prefer? Chances are it'll be the second. We will show you how to use the **Crop Tool** in combination with the **Thirds Grid** so that you can fine tune your composition before finally committing to a crop.

By the end of this tutorial you will be able to:

• Use the **Thirds Grid** when cropping to aid photo composition.

What is the Rule of Thirds?

This is both the photographer's and painter's favourite rule and its use was documented as early as 1757! The main reason for observing the Rule of Thirds is to ensure that your subject is not placed in the centre, and to prevent a horizon from appearing to divide the picture in half.

Our example image is a stunning sunset. However, the horizon divides the image in two and it looks quite static as the boat is positioned right in the centre.

Now let's apply a crop using the Rule of Thirds. To apply the Rule of Thirds you need to divide your photo into nine equal parts by the use of two equally spaced vertical lines and two equally spaced horizontal lines.

Your main subject of the photo (in this case the boat) should then be placed along one of the four intersections, known as Power Points. The horizon should ideally follow the line along either the lower third, or the upper third of the grid. Notice that the intense light of the sun also takes advantage of the rule as it's positioned along one of the vertical thirds.

This leads to a stronger composition, and a more aesthetically pleasing photograph.

Your images may not conform to this standard, but you can easily correct this in PhotoPlus. To find out how, see the **Cropping I** tutorial on p. 19.

Raw or JPEG?

To begin, let's look at the differences between JPEG and raw file formats.

What is JPEG?

JPEG (Joint Photographic Experts Group) is a type of **lossy compression** that is most suited to images that contain thousands of colours, namely photographs. Lossy compression means that some data is 'thrown away' each time the file is edited and saved. However, at high quality settings, the quality loss is undetectable to the human eye. This means that by saving to JPEG, you can save a significant amount of space and lose very little quality. JPEG files (*.jpg) are widely supported and as a result, are the file type of choice if you want to share your digital images.

In digital photography terms, the JPEG file is the finished article. All of the processing such as white balance, saturation, sharpness, contrast etc. is done by the camera. The JPEG file can be viewed and printed without any further editing. This is a big advantage as it can save time and money.

What is raw?

Unlike JPEG files, raw is not a file type! Raw files are simply files that contain the 'raw' data from the camera sensor. As a result, all raw files need some form of post-processing using image editing software such as PhotoPlus. Raw file types are manufacturer specific and cannot normally be displayed by a standard Windows browser. As a result, they must be converted to either JPEG or some other format before they can be shared.

You might be thinking that if you have to convert a raw file to a JPEG, then why waste the time shooting in raw to start with?

Shooting in raw has two advantages over JPEG. The first is that the processing is done via the computer. This means that you can change many of the shooting parameters **after** exposure. Instead of relying on the camera settings, you can manually alter the white balance, contrast, saturation, and sharpness. You can also recover some of the blown highlights caused by over-exposure. (See the **Raw I** tutorial on p. 61 for more information.) It is the best format if you're unsure of the conditions.

Raw files can also be converted to 8 or 16 bits/channel TIFF or HD photo files. The industry standard TIFF format creates a large file, but the **lossless compression** format makes them ideal for documents that are going to be frequently opened, edited and saved. (The HD photo format also uses a lossless compression when saved at 100% quality.) Perform multiple edits and saves with a JPEG, and you rapidly lose image quality.

Do I shoot in raw or JPEG?

The format you choose depends on what you are shooting and what you want to do with the image afterwards.

JPEG

JPEGs are smaller files than their raw counterparts. Not only do they take up less space on the memory card, they write to the card faster too. This makes JPEGs the only real option when you want to capture fast moving objects or when shooting in a continuous burst mode.

As we've said before, post-processing is not essential with a JPEG. If you know that you have the correct exposure and white balance, shoot a high quality JPEG. The workflow is faster and the end result will look just as good.

Raw

If you're not sure about the lighting, or if you know that you want to do some specialist post-processing on an image, shoot in raw. The 16 bit capability of raw files, the data they store and the capability to edit in a lossless way, allow you to make adjustments that are not possible with a JPEG. Raw files may take up more space, but they are the best option if you know you'll want to make substantial changes.

Raw + JPEG

Some cameras allow you to take both file formats simultaneously. While the extra write time means that this is not necessarily an option for sports events, this format gives you the best of both worlds: you have a JPEG image that you can quickly share or print, but you also have the editing capabilities of the raw file if the JPEG doesn't work out as planned. If the JPEGs are perfect, you can always delete the raw files at a later date to save space.

Understanding Masks

Masks are an infinitely useful tool to master. They allow you to make changes to photos and images quickly and easily in a totally non-destructive way. This is why masks are applied automatically when you add an adjustment layer. While they may look confusing, they are in fact extremely easy to use. We'll show you how in this tutorial by creating a photo montage.

By the end of this tutorial you will be able to:

- Create a mask from selection.

- Edit a mask.

In this tutorial, we will create a photo montage using three photos. We have provided the project file for you to use.

 Go to **http://go.serif.com/resources/HPX4** to download the following tutorial project file(s):

- **mask.spp**

Let's begin...

- On the Standard toolbar, click 📂 **Open**.

- Locate the **mask.spp** file and click **Open**.

    The image opens in the workspace.

If you look at the **Layers** tab, you'll see that this project contains three layers. Each layer contains a different image.

To create our montage, we need to erase parts of the top images to reveal the background. However, if we did this using the **Standard Eraser**, it would be really difficult to edit the image if we change our mind or make a mistake. This is where masks come in. Masks can be used to hide parts of an image (or effect) while revealing another part. Masks are easy to use and what's more, they make it really easy to change your mind! Let's get started.

You can add a blank, reveal all mask (white thumbnail) by simply clicking 🖼 **Add Layer Mask** on the **Layers** tab, however, it's often much easier to create one from a selection. You can always edit the mask later.

To create a mask from a standard selection:

1   On the **Layers** tab, select the 'Man' layer.

2   On the Tools toolbar, on the Selection Tools flyout, click the
    ○ **Ellipse Selection Tool** and on the context toolbar, set the
    Feather to **0**.

3   Drag the selection around the head and shoulders of the man. If
    necessary, move the selection into position.

    Let's feather the selection a little.

4   On the context toolbar, click **Modify Selection...**

5   In the dialog:

    •   Click **White Matte** in the Preview drop-down list. This
        will show us what part of the picture will be protected
        when we create the mask.

- Drag the **Feather** slider to the right until you get an effect you like—a feather of 45 works well.

- Click **OK**. The selection is updated.

7 On the **Layers** tab, click ⬚ **Add Layer Mask**. A mask thumbnail is added to the layer.

On the page, the selected area remains, whereas the area outside of the selection is hidden.

Our first mask is complete. If you temporarily hide the 'Ball and racquet' layer, you'll see that we've created a subtle edge to our photo montage. (Don't forget to make the 'Ball and racquet' layer visible again before attempting the next step.)

💡 You can view your mask at any time by clicking **Layers>Mask>View Mask** or by pressing the **Alt** key and clicking on the mask thumbnail on the **Layers** tab.

To create the second mask, we're going to use the 🖌 **Brush Selection Tool**. Before we start, if your previous selection is still active, press **Ctrl + D** to deselect it.

To create a mask from a selection II:

1   On the **Layers** tab, select the 'Ball and racquet' layer.

2   On the Tools toolbar, click the 🖌 **Brush Selection Tool** and on the **Brush Tip** tab, select the 64 pixel hard (**Round Hard07**) brush.

3   Paint over the ball and racquet to create a selection around the objects. Don't worry about being too accurate, we'll correct any mistakes later.

4   On the context toolbar, click **Modify Selection...**

5   In the dialog:

- Click **White Matte** in the Preview drop-down list. This will show us what part of the picture will be protected when we create the mask.

- Set the **Feather** to around 5 pixels.

- Click **OK**. The selection is updated.

6   On the **Layers** tab, click  **Add Layer Mask**.

The mask is added to the layer and the background is revealed.

We're almost finished, however, if your image is like ours, you'll notice that there is a little too much fade around the edge of the ball and racquet. We can easily fix this by editing the mask. First of all, we need to remove the current selection. Either press **Ctrl + D** or go to **Select > Deselect**.

To edit a mask:

1   On the **Layers** tab, the 'Ball and racquet' mask thumbnail should be selected (surrounded by a white outline). If not, click once to select it.

2   On the **Colour** tab, notice that the colours have automatically changed to black and white. The foreground swatch should already be white, if not, set it to white now.

3   On the Tools toolbar, click the ✎ **Paintbrush Tool** and on the **Brush Tip** tab, select the 64 pixel soft brush.

4   Carefully start to paint around the edges of the racquet and ball. If
    you make a mistake, switch the foreground back to black and paint
    over the mistake to reapply the mask. Also, fill in any holes that may
    have been in your selection.

Next, we'll blend the left edge of the photo into the background.
We'll do this with the gradient tool.

5   On the Tools toolbar, on the Selection Tools flyout, click the
    ⬚ **Rectangle Selection Tool** and on the context toolbar, set the
    Feather to **0**.

6   Click and drag on the lower-left portion of the image to create a
    small selection, taking care to ensure that it touches the bottom edge
    of the image.

7   On the Tools toolbar, in the Fill flyout, click the ▥ **Gradient Fill
    Tool**. On the context toolbar, the gradient should be set as a black
    to white linear gradient. (If not, click the gradient swatch and then in
    the dialog, click the first gradient swatch.)

8   Starting in the centre, drag the gradient from left to right.

On release, the gradient is applied to the selection.

If you are happy with the gradient, press **Ctrl + D** to deselect.

9   You'll notice that there is now a hard line just above the shadow. Click the ✏ **Paintbrush Tool** and on the **Colour** tab, switch the foreground to black.

10 Carefully paint over the edge to soften it.

That's it! Your photo montage is complete!

Retouching

How often have you taken a photo, only to have it spoiled by a cluttered background or other blemishes? Sometimes, it's unavoidable. However, with PhotoPlus you can remove unwanted objects easily. We'll show you how to use the clone and repair tools to do just that in this tutorial.

By the end of this tutorial you will be able to:

- Use the **Scratch Remover** tool to remove small blemishes.

- Add a new layer and remove unwanted objects using the **Clone Tool**.

To help you to complete the tutorial, we've provided our starting photo.

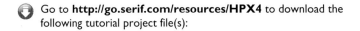 Go to **http://go.serif.com/resources/HPX4** to download the following tutorial project file(s):

◎ **puppy.jpg**

Let's begin...

- On the Standard toolbar, click  **Open**.

- Locate the **puppy.jpg** (or your own photo) and click **Open**.

  The image opens in the workspace.

If you zoom in to the dog's face (using the 🔍 **Zoom Tool**), you'll notice that there are a couple of white spots near the eyes.

We can easily fix these by using the **Scratch Remover**. First, we'll create a duplicate layer, just in case we make any mistakes.

To create a duplicate layer:

1 On the **Layers** tab, right-click the 'Background' layer and in the menu, click **Duplicate...**

2 In the dialog, click **OK** to accept the default settings. An exact copy of the 'Background' layer is displayed in the **Layers** tab.

To remove small blemishes:

1 On the Tools toolbar, on the Blemish Tools flyout, click the ❀ **Scratch Remover**.

2 On the **Brush Tip** tab, in the **Basic** brush category, choose a 16 pixel soft brush tip.

3 On the Context toolbar, select the **Aligned** check box.

The **Aligned** option affects what happens if you use more than one brush stroke. In aligned mode, subsequent clicks resample the clone source from the surrounding area. In non-aligned mode, subsequent clicks take the pixels from the original clone source.

4   To define the clone source, hold down the **Shift** key and click a spot near to the white blemish. This samples the area under the brush.

5   Release the **Shift** key and click to paint over the white mark—it should blend into the surrounding area.

6   Repeat step 4 and 5 to remove any other small marks on the face.

Our work with the **Scratch Remover** is complete! The next step is to remove the background clutter. For this we need the ♟ **Clone Tool**.

When cloning parts of an image, it's always best practice to work on a new layer. This makes it much easier to correct mistakes and also protects the original image.

To use the Clone Tool:

1   On the **Layers** tab, click ⊞ **New Layer**. In the **Layer Properties** dialog, name the layer 'Cloned Area.'

We'll now use an area of 'clean' grass on the left of the photo to clone over the clutter and take it out of the picture.

2   On the Tools toolbar, click the 🖳 **Clone Tool**. On the Context toolbar:

- Increase the brush **Size** to about **50** pix.

- Select the **Use all layers** option.

- Select the **Aligned** option (so that each new stroke lines up with the previous one).

🖱   You may want to alternate between Aligned and Non-aligned modes when retouching your photo. There are no hard and fast rules.

3   We're going to start by removing the box next to the dog. Zoom in to this area using the 🔍 **Zoom Tool**.

4   **Shift**-click on an area of grass that matches the depth of field to define the clone source for the new area.

5 On the 'Cloned Area' layer, make your first clone stroke. If the grass doesn't seem to match properly, **Shift**-click on another area to redefine the clone source.

6 As the area we're removing is bigger than the area we're sampling you'll have to reset the position of the **Clone Tool** a few times. This is good practice as it also helps to reduce repeated patterns.

7 To remove the area near the ear and close to the body, reduce the brush size and redefine the clone area again. Don't worry if you paint over the dog, because we are cloning to a separate layer, you will be able to erase any mistakes later.

8 Finally, to ensure that the cloned area looks slightly different, reduce the brush **Opacity** to around **20%**, **Shift**-click on a brighter area of grass above the area you are working, and paint over the cloned area again. Any patterning should be removed and will look more natural.

Retouching

9   Repeat the steps above to clone out the other distractions.
     Remember to always define a clone source that matches the depth of
     field and colour of the surrounding background. This way the end
     result will look more natural.

Finishing touches

If you have accidentally cloned the background over the top of the dog,
you simply need to erase the cloned area with the ✏ **Standard Eraser**.

💡   You can save yourself a lot of frustration in this stage by
     following this tip! Before you start to erase anything, on
     the **Layers** tab, change the blend mode of the 'Cloned
     area' layer to **Screen**. If needed you can also reduce the
     opacity until you can see the outline of the dog beneath.

     When you've finished, simply reset the blend mode made
     to **Normal** at 100% opacity!

Your final image should resemble ours. Don't forget to export it to a new image!

Your retouching projects can be as ambitious as you want. Our final examples use the techniques described here, in combination with some other techniques that can be found within the tutorials.

> 💡 If you need to 'blend' cloned areas, you might also want to have a look at the 🔵 **Patch Tool**. For more information, see Help.

Example 1:

Example 2:

Good luck!

Raw 1: The Raw Studio

When you save a photo as a raw file, you are essentially saving an unprocessed image. It's basically a digital negative and needs to be developed. PhotoPlus has a digital dark room equivalent and it's called Raw Studio.

The first image is a screen capture of the raw file as it is displayed using the stored camera settings. As you can see, the image is suffering from blown highlights, colour balance and saturation problems. In this tutorial, we'll look at some basic corrections and settings that you apply to your raw file in Raw Studio.

Using the Raw Studio

There are many types of raw files, in fact, most camera manufacturers have their own file type. The image we'll use to demonstrate Raw Studio is a slightly over-exposed image of a swan. Unfortunately, as raw files are so large, we can't provide our image for you to use, but the steps in the tutorial will work with any image with similar exposure problems. Remember, there are no hard and fast rules. Corrections are mainly done by eye and need to be adjusted to each individual photo.

By the end of this tutorial you will be able to:

- Open a raw image file.

- Adjust white balance.

- Recover blown highlights.

- Alter exposure.

- Reduce noise.

To open a raw image:

- Click **Open** on the Standard toolbar and then browse to your raw file.

    - or -

- Drag and drop a raw file from Windows Explorer onto the empty workspace.

The image opens in Raw Studio.

Let's start with the first correction.

🐾 The corrected image will always be displayed on the right in the image. Note that this displays the cumulative effect of all of the applied adjustments.

Our image of the swan has a blue cast. We can see this in the feathers and by looking at the histogram.

To correct the white balance:

1 In the **Colour and Tone** section, click the ✦ **Colour Picker**.

2 Click on a white area of your image to create a neutral reference point.

The colour balance is updated. If it's not quite right, click on another area until a natural colour balance is achieved.

Notice that the histogram is also updated to show the change in tonal balance.

If we look closely at the right side of the histogram, we can see that there is a peak right at the edge. This tells us that the image has blown highlights.

Raw files store a little extra data about exposure. This means that if an image was slightly over-exposed, you can recover a certain amount of the exposure data. We can either change the exposure or use **highlight recovery**.

To recover highlights:

1   In the **Highlights** section, select **Recovery** from the **Mode** drop-down menu.

2   Begin with **Strength** setting of I and gradually increase it until the detail starts to appear in the blown section.

The entire image will get darker, but we can correct this later.

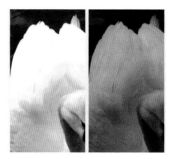

At a strength of 2, the detail has appeared in the feathers of the swan. Notice that the histogram has been squashed so that there is no longer any clipping. There is now a lot of space to the right of the histogram.

As you increase the highlight recovery strength, you may introduce colour casting. However, this can easily be fixed by a Colour Balance adjustment in PhotoPlus.

We can balance the histogram again by adjusting the exposure.

To lighten the image:

1   In the **Colour and Tone** section, drag the **Exposure** slider to the right.

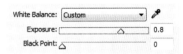

2   Aim for small increments and let the preview pane update each time before you make further adjustments.

3   Keep an eye on the histogram and make sure that you stop before clipping occurs at the right edge.

Notice that the histogram has spread out again while retaining the shape it had after highlight recovery. We still have a small amount of space to the right but this can be fixed later with a **Levels** adjustment in PhotoPlus.

This image is almost finished. However, it could benefit from a low level noise reduction.

To reduce noise:

- In the **Noise Reduction** section, gradually increase the **Strength** until you get the desired effect.

  Stop before you noticeably lose detail.

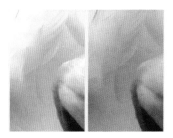

When you are happy with your image, click **OK** to exit **Raw Studio**.

The image opens in the PhotoPlus workspace.

We think you'll agree that this is a vast improvement on the original image.

Saving your image

The next steps are entirely up to you. However, before you go any further you should save your image. There are several options open to you.

Save as a project

If you want to make adjustments and keep the layers editable, save your image as a PhotoPlus project (recommended).

Export to a common file format

You can export your image to various file formats via the **Export Optimizer** (from the **File** menu).

Each format has its advantages:

- If you need to make further adjustments to your 16 bit depth file, you should export to a 16 bits/channel lossless compression format, such as 48 or 64 bit TIFF.

- If you want to apply effects and filters, export to an 8 bits/channel lossless compression format, such as 24 or 32 bit TIFF and PNG. These files can be used as an intermediate as they can be edited and saved repeatedly without loss in quality.

- If you do not intend to edit and resave your file more than once or twice, export to a JPEG. A high quality JPEG is the best format to use when sharing, printing or archiving files as the file size is much smaller than the same quality TIFF or PNG. Remember, JPEG is a lossy compression format, so there will be some loss of quality each time a JPEG image is edited and resaved.

Raw II: Workflow

This tutorial expands on the **Raw I: The Raw Studio** tutorial (p. 61) and introduces common post-processing workflow. Hopefully, we'll also give you some creative inspiration and help you to create stunning photo prints!

By the end of this tutorial you will be able to:

*   Understand a typical photo workflow.

*   Apply creative effects to enhance a photo.

In this tutorial we hope to give you some creative inspiration. However, we won't go into detail as the techniques are covered in detail in many of the other tutorials.

Typical image workflow

It's a rare thing to have a photo that doesn't require some form of adjustment, and raw files always need some form of conversion. A typical photo workflow would include some or all of the following:

- Convert raw files (**Raw Studio**)

- Straighten

- Curves and Levels adjustment

- Cloning out unwanted areas

- Noise reduction

- Crop

- Sharpen

- Add filters to add artistic flare!

- Share!

The first set of adjustments is applied to a 16 bit depth file. Later on, we'll need to convert to an 8 bit depth file to apply some of the other adjustments and effects.

Levels and Curves

Our swan image was still a little dark and had areas of uneven tone. To correct this we applied several small **Levels** and **Curves** adjustments layers. We used the ✎ **Magic Wand Tool** and the ♀ **Freehand Selection Tool** to create selections around the problem areas. When the adjustment layer was added, PhotoPlus only applied the adjustment to the active selection.

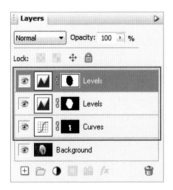

For more information on **Levels** and **Curves** adjustment layers, see the **Key Adjustments** tutorial (p. 7).

Black and White

We felt that the swan image would work well as a black and white print.
Although there are several ways to do this in PhotoPlus, we used a
Channel Mixer adjustment layer.

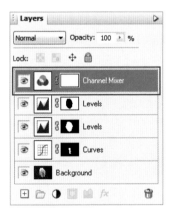

See the **Making Monochrome Images** (p. 91) and **Popping Colour**
(p. 115) tutorials for details.

Crop

We used the ⊡ **Crop Tool** to give our image an artistic, square crop.

For more information on image cropping, see **Cropping I** tutorial for details (p. 19).

Sharpen

Raw images often look a little 'soft' as no in-camera sharpening is applied. We applied an **Unsharp Mask** filter layer (see **Key Adjustments** on p. 7 for details).

At this point, we have an image that's ready to print and share. We could export it as a high quality JPEG for printing and archiving, or we could resize it for the Web.

We wanted to be a little more artistic and chose to add a depth of field effect. However, as many of the filter effects only work on an 8 bit depth file, we had to convert our 16 bits/channel image to 8 bits/channel.

Convert to 8 bits/channel

There are several ways to do this in PhotoPlus, but it is often best to create a new file. We used the **Export Optimizer** to export our image as a 24 bit TIFF which we then opened in PhotoPlus.

Depth of Field Effect

To complete our image, we created a filter layer to add a **Depth of Field** effect.

To add a radial Depth of Field effect:

1   On the **Layers** tab, right-click the layer containing your image and then click **Duplicate**. In the **Duplicate Layer** dialog, name your layer and click **OK**.

2   Right click the new layer and click **Convert to Filter Layer...**

3   In the **Filter Gallery**, open the **Blur** category and click the **Depth of Field** thumbnail.

4   Click ⊕ Set Path then, in the preview pane, adjust the gradient path to create the direction of the blur.

     We set the path so the focal point was over the swan's head and the greatest blur intensity was at the edge of the swan's body.

🖎   The square node controls the focal point of the **Depth of Field** blur whereas the circular node controls the blur.

5   In the **Depth of Field** settings:

   *   Set the **Blur Radius** (the amount of blur).

   *   Set the **Focal Distance** (the distance from the gradient
       focal point).

   *   Set the **Depth Map** to **Radial Gradient**.

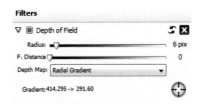

6   Click **OK** to apply the settings and exit.

Export to high quality JPEG

Our final step was to export our image as a high quality JPEG ready for
archiving, printing and sharing.

To export an image:

1   On the **File** menu, select **Export Optimizer...**.

2   In the **Export Optimizer** dialog:

- Set the **Format** to **JPG**.

- Set the **Quality** to **95%**.

- Click **Export**.

3   In the **Export** dialog, type a name for your file and click **OK**.

Your JPEG image is saved to the location you specified and ready to print and share!

💡   Reducing the quality of a JPEG to 95% can result in a file size that is half the size of a JPEG exported at 100%! Providing this is the first time you've created a JPEG, the loss in image quality is virtually undetectable to the human eye.

Macros and Batch Processing

Following a holiday or special occasion it's only natural to want to share the experience with friends and family by showing them the photos you've taken. Chances are they are either too big, take up too much disk space, or are the wrong file format.

In this tutorial we will show you how PhotoPlus's macro and batch processing capabilities can be combined to easily solve these problems.

By the end of this tutorial you will be able to:

- Resize an image quickly and easily using a macro.

- Use batch processing to apply your macro to multiple images.

Let's begin...

Before we start this exercise, let's take some time out to explain exactly what we mean by 'macro.'

A macro is simply a saved sequence of steps (for example, commands, keyboard strokes, or mouse clicks) that you can store and then recall later with a single command or keyboard stroke. Macros are particularly useful for multi-step tasks that are carried out repeatedly, or complex procedures that are time consuming to reproduce—simply record the steps once, then replay the recording whenever you like.

Macros

Now we know what a macro is, let's create one...

To create a macro:

1   Click the **Macros** tab.

- On the **Macros** tab, click  **New Category**. In the **Category** dialog, in the **Name** box, type 'My Macros.' Click **OK**.

- In the **Macros** tab category list, ensure that **My Macros** is the selected category, and then click the ⊞ **New Macro** button. In the **New Macro** dialog, enter the name for the macro as 'My Resize.' Click **OK**.

    You have just created the **My Resize** macro in the **My Macros** category. Your **Macros** tab should now look like ours.

2   Now that we have our category and empty macro set up, we can start recording our macro steps.

We want our macro to help us resize images, so we will need to record specific values in the **Image Size** dialog.

Most of PhotoPlus's functionality is available only with an open image. Therefore, before we can record a macro, we need to open an image.

When creating macros, it's worthwhile jotting down on paper what you want to record in your macro before you actually begin recording. This will save a lot of potential mistakes. Additionally, it doesn't matter how long you take to carry out the steps you are recording; PhotoPlus will record only the commands carried out, not the time taken to do so.

3   On the **File** menu, click **New...**

Create a new image of default dimensions.

On the **Macros** tab, with the **My Resize** macro selected, click the **Start Recording** button.

4   On the **Image** menu, select **Image Size**. In the **Image Size** dialog:

• Make sure that the **Resize Layers** and **Maintain aspect ratio** check boxes are selected.

• In the **Pixel Size** section, change the units to **percent**, and enter **50** for the **Width**. As you have Maintain aspect ratio selected, the **Height** will automatically update.

• Click **OK**.

We used the default Resampling method for our macro example, but you might want to adjust this depending on the image quality required for your resulting images.

5   That is all we need to record, so back on the **Macros** tab, click **Stop Recording**.

Note: You must click **Stop Recording** when you have finished performing all the steps you want in your macro, otherwise you will be adding actions to it that you may not want!

At this point, you may be thinking that since we had to enter settings into a dialog, each time we run the macro, that same dialog will be displayed and will require input. This does not have to be the case, as we'll now show you.

6   On the **Macros** tab, click the arrow to the left of **My Resize**.

This expands the macro to show each of the constituent steps included. In our case we have just the one step, automatically labelled **Image Size** due to displaying the **Image Size** dialog.

Here, we can enable or disable constituent steps in the dialog by adding or removing a check mark: you will see that **Image Size** is enabled by default in our macro.

We can also choose whether to show any dialog that may be associated with a constituent step. The default (and the best option here) is to not show the dialog each time the macro is run; you can change this if desired by clicking to add or remove the check mark.

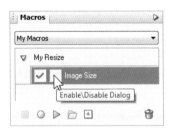

Now we have our macro, let's test it.

To use a macro:

1   On the Standard toolbar, click 🗁 **Open**. Then, locate your chosen photo and click **Open**.

The image opens in the workspace.

2   On the **Macros** tab, ensure **My Resize** is the selected macro, then click the ▷ **Play** button. Instantly, the image is resized to 50% of its original dimensions, and will now only occupy roughly half the disk space when saved.

Batch processing

Although this macro works perfectly well on individual images, the real power of it is not exposed until it is used in conjunction with batch processing. Batch processing gives us the capability to process several images in a similar way, all in one step. In our case, we would like to be able to apply our macro to several images that all need resizing. PhotoPlus provides a method to do just that!

To use a macro as part of a batch process:

1   On the **File** menu, select **Batch...**

The **Batch** dialog lets us use a macro in the batch process if required, which is just what we want. We can also specify the output file type, the folder that contains all the images to be processed, and the folder that is to contain all the processed images.

2   In the **Batch** dialog:

- Select the **Use Macro** check box.

- In the **Category** drop-down list, select **My Macros**.

- In the **Macro** list, select **My Resize** (currently the only macro in the list).

- Select the **Change File Type** check box, and select **JPEG** as the format.

- In the **Source Folder** section, click **Browse** and then browse to a folder containing images you want to resize.

  Select the folder and then click **OK**.

- In the **Destination** section, click **Browse**. Create a new folder in a convenient location, say **C:\Resized Images**.

- At the bottom of the dialog, click **Modify**.

  The **File Name Format** dialog opens. Here, we can specify how each processed file is to be labelled.

3   In the **Tokens** pane, select **Document Name** and then click **Add**.

- Select **Text** and then click **Add**. A **Text** box displays beneath the **Format** pane. In the box, type '_small.' This ensures that each processed image will have a filename consisting of its original filename, followed by _**small**.

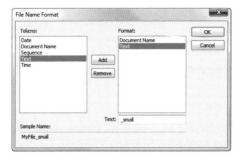

- Click **OK** to close the **File Name Format** dialog.

4   Back in the **Batch** dialog, all our settings are complete, so click **OK** to run the batch process.

  You will see PhotoPlus open each image in the specified source folder, apply the macro, and then close the image.

5   Browse to the folder you specified as your destination folder. You will see that all the images there have been reduced in dimensions by 50%, and are now JPG in format.

  Compare the time taken to apply this batch process with how long it would take to open each image, display the **Image Size** dialog, specify the new dimensions, and then export the image as a JPG.

To resize multiple images and run a macro simultaneously, you can also use the **Resize Image** functionality included in the **Batch** dialog.

Macros and Batch Processing

To run a macro while resizing images:

1 Set up your batch process as described previously (p. 85); keep the **Batch Processing** dialog open.

2 In addition, select the **Resize Images** checkbox.

3 Adjust the settings in the **Resize Images** section.

4 Click **OK**.

This tutorial has focused on combining a custom macro with a batch process to resize a collection of images. However, the **Macros** tab provides an extensive selection of predefined macros. With these you can quickly and easily enhance, manipulate, and apply creative effects to a single image, or, when used in a batch process, to multiple images.

In the example, we applied a hand sketched effect with the **Effects** category's **Soft Pastel** macro.

For more information on macros, see the **Making Monochrome Images** tutorial (p. 91) or PhotoPlus Help.

Creative effects

In this set of tutorials, we'll focus on the fantastic artistic effects created by adjusting, adding or removing colours, embellishing photos by adding extra graphics, and changing the weather to improve atmosphere.

Making Monochrome Images

Monochrome (black and white) images can look sophisticated, artistic and modern. What's more, a poor quality colour image can often be rescued by turning it into a great looking monochrome image! With a digital image and PhotoPlus, it's easy to make great-looking monochrome images. The best part is that you'll never need to know where the monochrome setting is on your camera, in fact, your images will probably be even better if you don't!

By the end of this tutorial you will be able to:

- Apply and adjust a **Channel Mixer** adjustment.

- Apply and adjust a **Black and White Film** adjustment.

- Create a monochrome image using a layer blend mode.

- Apply and adjust a **Hue/Saturation/Lightness** adjustment.

- Convert an image to greyscale.

- Use the **Black & White Photography** macros.

To illustrate the following effects, we've used pictures taken at the 2010 Isle of Man TT, as we think you'll agree that they make very dynamic monochrome images.

Don't forget that other tools, such as 🔧 Dodge and 🖐 Burn will also be on hand to allow you to make further subtle contrast adjustments (see the **How To** tab for more information) in combination with any of the following methods.

Go to **http://go.serif.com/resources/HPX4** to download the following tutorial project file(s):

TT2010_38.jpg

TT2010_68.jpg

Let's begin...

- On the Standard toolbar, click 🗁 **Open**.

- Locate your chosen photo (or use the ones provided) and click **Open**.

  The image opens in the workspace.

Channel Mixer

The **Channel Mixer** adjustment can produce one of the best monochrome effects, leading to high contrast images. The best way to start off is to identify which channel has the best contrast to start off with.

To view individual channels:

- On the **Channels** tab, click either the **Red**, **Green** or **Blue** channel. The corresponding image channel is displayed in the workspace and the channel is highlighted on the **Channels** tab.

- Click **RGB** to return to full colour.

As you can see from the screenshot below, the different channels produce quite different effects.

In this case, the best channel for contrast purposes is the green channel. We'll use this channel for our **Channel Mixer** adjustment.

To add a Channel Mixer adjustment:

1   On the **Adjustments** tab, click **Channel Mixer...**

A new adjustment layer is added to the **Layers** tab.

2   In the **Adjustments** tab:

• Set the **Output Channel** to **Green**.

• Select the **Monochrome** option.

The **Output Channel** updates to display **Black**.

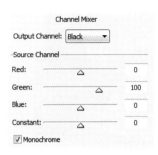

3   To boost contrast even more, drag the sliders of each individual
     channel until you get an effect that you like.

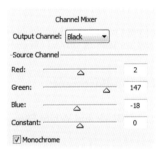

The **Channel Mixer** adjustment is great to use with a colour pop
effect! For more on how to do this, see the **Popping Colour**
tutorial on p. 115.

Black and White Film

The **Black and White Film** adjustment is both quick to apply and easy to adjust. You can get some great and sometimes surreal effects!

To apply a Black and White Film adjustment:

1   On the **Adjustments** tab, click **Black and White Film...**

A new adjustment layer is added to the **Layers** tab.

An 'optimized' black and white effect is produced.

If you like this effect, you'll need no further changes. However, to tweak the contrast of the various colours, you can use the **Adjustments** tab.

2   On the **Adjustments** tab, drag the various colour sliders to the left or right to either boost or reduce contrast.

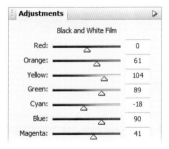

3   To apply a colour tint, on the **Adjustments** tab, select the **Tint** option. Drag the **Hue** slider to choose the tint colour and control the tint saturation with the **Saturation** slider.

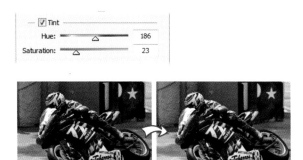

Using layer blend modes

Layer blend modes can be used to quickly change a colour image to black and white. As you are working on a separate layer, it's a completely non-destructive approach and makes it easy to create other artistic effects, such as a creating colour pop by applying a mask.

To convert photo to monochrome using Blend Modes:

1   On the **Layers** tab, click the ⊞ **New Layer** and in the dialog rename the layer 'B&W'.

2   On the **Colour** tab, click ▪ **Reset Colours**. The foreground swatch is set to black while the background swatch is set to white.

3   On the Tools toolbar, on the Fill Tools flyout, select the ◈ **Flood Fill Tool** and then click inside the new layer to fill it.

4   On the **Layers** tab, set the **Blend Mode** to **Colour**.

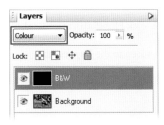

That's it! Your image is immediately converted to monochrome!

We've used this approach to reduce colour saturation of our image in the **Weather Effects** tutorials (see p. 139). You can easily create sepia or tinted effects by using an additional, coloured layer on top of the 'B&W' layer and again using a Colour blend.

Hue/Saturation/Lightness (HSL) adjustment

You can quickly convert an image to greyscale using a Hue/Saturation/Lightness adjustment layer. It is a useful adjustment as it retains all channels and allows various effects to be created. However, overall fine-tuning using this method is limited and the result can end up looking flat.

Making Monochrome Images

To apply an HSL adjustment:

1   On the **Adjustments** tab, click **Hue/Saturation/Lightness...**

A new adjustment layer is added to the **Layers** tab.

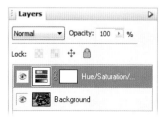

2   In the **Adjustments** tab, drag the Saturation slider all the way to the left (-100) to completely desaturate the appearance of the underlying layers.

Greyscale

This is the option that most people will think of when they want to create a black and white image. However, while it has the advantages of being really quick and creating a small file size, it doesn't necessarily produce the best results as the image can often look flat.

⚠   Converting to greyscale is a destructive approach to creating a monochrome image, so ensure that you use a copy of the file.

To convert to greyscale:

- On the **Image** menu, click **Colour Mode > Greyscale** (8 bit for jpg files, 16 bit for Raw).

Notice that after the conversion, the **Channels** tab displays a single channel.

Also, the **Colour** tab will only show Black and White with the option to adjust lightness.

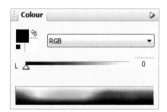

This will remain the case until you close and reopen the file. You will have to reopen the file if you want to add any colour back into your image. However, other tools, such as ✎ **Dodge** and ✎ **Burn** will always be available to allow you to make contrast adjustments (see the **How To** tab for more information).

Macros

PhotoPlus provides a range of preset macros which you can use to apply various greyscale effects to an image with a single click.

To apply preset monochrome macros:

1   On the **Macros** tab, select the **Black & White Photography** category in the drop-down list.

2   Select the macro you want to run, and then click ▷ **Play**.

3   The macro is applied to your image.

Examples

To give you an idea of what the various macros can achieve, we've applied some of the **Black & White Photography** macros to some more motorcycle racing images.

Green Filter macro (A), Red Filter macro (B) and Infrared (Dreamy) macro (C).

Recolouring Images

Ever wanted to change the colour of your car without the risk and expense? Try it first with a photo! PhotoPlus provides several ways to selectively replace colour in an image—a useful technique to have in your armoury! In this tutorial, we'll show you how to do it in a non-destructive way by using filters, layers and masks.

By the end of this tutorial you will be able to:

- Create a freehand selection.

- Change colour using a **Hue/Saturation/Lightness** adjustment.

- Use the **Colour Pickup Tool** to select a foreground colour.

- Use the **Paintbrush Tool** in combination with a **Colour** blend mode to selectively apply colour.

- Select and edit a mask.

Go to **http://go.serif.com/resources/HPX4** to download the following tutorial project file(s):

○ **car.jpg**

Let's begin...

- On the Standard toolbar, click 📂 **Open**.

- Locate the **car.jpg** and click **Open**.

Our car is a single colour, in this case red. This means that we can easily change its colour by adjusting the **Hue**. However, as there may be reds in other parts of the image, we need to protect those areas in some way. We can do this by using a mask. Luckily, we can get PhotoPlus to do most of the job for us. All we need to do is create a selection of the part we want to change before adding an **Adjustment** layer. Let's do this now.

To create a selection:

1   On the Tools toolbar, on the Selection flyout, click the
    ♀ **Freehand Selection Tool**.

2   On the context toolbar, set the **Feather** to **0**.

3   Click and drag to draw a selection around the red body of the car.
    Don't worry about being too accurate at this stage as we can make
    corrections later.

Next, we need to add our **Adjustment** layer.

To add a Hue/Saturation/Lightness adjustment:

1   On the **Adjustments** tab, click **Hue/Saturation/Lightness**.

A new adjustment layer is added and displayed in the **Layers** tab. Notice that a mask has been automatically created from your selection.

2   On the **Adjustments** tab:

•   In the **Edit** drop-down list, select **Reds** to adjust the range of red tones in the image (if you leave the setting at **Master**, you will adjust the entire range).

•   Using the sliders (or by directly typing in the value) set the **Hue** value to **55,** the **Saturation** to **10** and the **Lightness** to **5**.

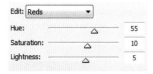

The deep red paintwork changes to yellow.

- In the **Range** spectrum, you'll see a set of 'range indicator' sliders in the red region, between the two spectrum bars.

These slider pairs show the affected colour ranges at each setting. Drag the sliders so that they approximately match the illustration below.

This expands the new colour range to include more shades of red, creating a more 'feathered' effect rather than a hard-edged tone.

You now have an image of a yellow sports car. Notice that when we applied the Hue/Saturation/Lightness (HSL) adjustment the lights of the car were also affected. We can easily correct this by editing the layer selection mask.

To edit a mask:

1   On the **Layers** tab, on the Hue/Saturation/Lightness adjustment layer, click to select the mask thumbnail. (A white border appears around the thumbnail to indicate that it is selected.)

2   On the **Colour** tab, notice that the colours have automatically changed to black and white. Click ■ to reset the swatches.

3   Click the 🖌 **Paintbrush Tool** and then, on the **Brush Tip** tab, choose the size **32** soft (*round06*) brush tip from the **Basic** category.

     On the Brush context toolbar, make sure that the **Blend** mode is set to **Normal** and the **Opacity** is set to **100%**.

4   With the brush colour set to black, carefully paint over the lights of the car. You'll notice that the original red colour will begin to show through as the mask is applied.

Recolouring Images

We also cleaned up other areas of the car, such as the number plate and the soft-top roof.

💡 If you make a mistake and remove too much of the mask, don't panic! Change the brush colour to white and paint over the mistake.

5 As the rear light is on, it will create a reflection on the paintwork. Set the **Opacity** of the brush to 20% and paint over the mask. This allows enough of the red to show through to create a realistic reflection, without spoiling the effect too much.

You'll have noticed that the bodywork still contains a few areas with a reddish tint, which weren't adjusted by the HSL adjustment layer. This is because the colour didn't fall exactly within the range we set in the dialog.

We'll fix these next...

To add a colour blend layer:

1   On the **Layers** tab, click ⊞ **New Layer** and in the dialog, rename the layer **C** (for Colour) and set the **Blend Mode** to **Colour**.

2   On the Tools toolbar, click the 🖊 **Colour Pickup Tool** and then click over an area of mid-yellow on the bodywork to make it the foreground colour.

(To verify this, check the foreground swatch on the **Colour** tab (ours is set to RGB 242, 216, 22.)

3 Click the ✐ **Paintbrush Tool** and then, on the context toolbar, make sure the blend mode is set to **Normal** and set the **Opacity** to **100%**.

Paint over the areas of the bodywork that need to be recoloured. If necessary, change the brush size on the context toolbar to match the area that you are working on.

💡 As you are working on a layer, any mistakes can be corrected with the ✐ **Standard Eraser Tool**.

You should now have a nice, shiny new paint job!

The HSL adjustment layer can be used in the same way to create a variety of different colours.

The best thing to do is to experiment as much as possible with a variety of different images. Have fun!

Popping Colour

Have you ever seen black and white photos with only a small portion of the photo appearing in colour? The technique is known as colour popping, and is an effective way of drawing the viewer's attention to the key focal points in the frame. The best part is that in PhotoPlus this is really easy to do, and in this tutorial, we'll show you how.

By the end of this tutorial you will be able to:

- Create a colour pop effect using an adjustment layer and a mask. (For more information about masking in general, see the **Understanding Masks** tutorial on p. 43.)

You can easily use any photo for this technique, but we've also provided the tutorial file for you to use.

 Go to **http://go.serif.com/resources/HPX4** to download the following tutorial project file(s):

○ **guitar.jpg**

Let's begin...

- On the Standard toolbar, click  **Open**.

- Locate the **guitar.jpg** (or your own photo) and click **Open**.

  The image opens in the workspace.

As this is a colour image, the first thing we need to do is apply an adjustment layer to allow us to create a black and white image while retaining the RGB channels. For more detail on this and other ways of creating a monochrome photo, see the **Making Monochrome Images** tutorial on p. 91. You can also use the **Black & White Studio** in the **How To** tab to apply many of the commands automatically.

To add a Channel Mixer adjustment:

1   On the **Adjustments** tab, click **Channel Mixer...**

    A new adjustment layer is added to the **Layers** tab.

2   On the **Adjustments** tab:

- Set the **Output Channel** to **Green**.

- Select the **Monochrome** option.

  The **Output Channel** updates to display **Black**.

Now we have an ideal high contrast black and white image, let's add some colour!

Using a mask

To create the colour pop, we need to reveal some of the original image. When you add an adjustment layer, a mask is automatically created for that layer (notice the white thumbnail).

All we need to do is paint on the mask to reveal the layer beneath. Let's do this now.

To reveal colour:

1   On the **Layers** tab, click to select the white mask thumbnail.

2   On the **Colour** tab, click ▪ **Reset Colours**. The foreground swatch is set to black while the background swatch is set to white.

3   On the Tools toolbar, click the ✎ **Paintbrush Tool**.

4   On the **Brush Tip** tab, in the **Basic** brush types list, you'll find soft and hard brushes, listed in that order. Choose an appropriate size soft brush tip. (We chose a 64 pixel brush.)

5   Start painting around the body of the guitar. Notice that the colour from the layer beneath is revealed as black is painted on the mask.

Don't worry about being too accurate with the paintbrush at this stage—we can easily fix any mistakes in the next step.

6   To paint inside the tricky areas, either select a smaller brush tip from the **Brush Tip** tab, or reduce the size using the Brush context toolbar.

When you've finished painting on the mask, you should have an image similar to ours.

Notice that there are some areas of colour that we don't want revealed (such as on the hands and the shirt). Let's fix this now.

7   On the **Colour** tab, click ✎ **Switch Colours**. The foreground swatch is set to white while the background swatch is set to black.

Popping Colour

8   Paint over the areas where you want to hide the colour again. (Use the 🔍 **Zoom Tool** to zoom in if you need to.)

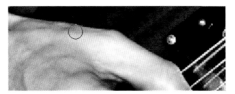

Once you've finished tidying up the masked areas, your colour pop is complete!

This technique can be used on all types of images, for example, this macro shot of a bee.

Some images are better suited to this technique than others, there are no hard fast rules so the best thing to do is to experiment for yourself. Have fun!

Adding Colour

Add a splash of colour to greyscale images—turn a photo into a modern, stylish digital creation. This relatively simple tutorial shows the ease with which colour can be added to a greyscale image.

By the end of this tutorial you will be able to:

- Add colour to an image using a layer blend mode.

You can easily use any photo for this technique, but we've also provided the tutorial file for you to use.

Go to **http://go.serif.com/resources/HPX4** to download the following tutorial project file(s):

⊙ **baby.jpg**

Let's begin...

- On the Standard toolbar, click 🗁 **Open**.

- Locate the **baby.jpg** (or your own photo) and click **Open**.

  The image opens in the workspace.

As this is a colour image, the first thing we need to do is apply an adjustment layer to allow us to create a black and white image while retaining the RGB channels. For more detail on this and other ways of creating a monochrome photo, see the **Making Monochrome Images** tutorial (p. 91). You can also use the **Black & White Studio** in the **How To** tab to apply many of the commands automatically.

To add a Black and White Film adjustment:

- On the **Adjustments** tab, click **Black and White Film...**

  A new adjustment layer is added to the **Layers** tab.

Now we have a black and white image, let's add some colour.

To paint colour on an image:

1   On the **Layers** tab, click the ⊞ **New Layer** button to add a new layer.

In the **Layer Properties** dialog:

- Name your layer 'Colour.'

- Set the **Blend Mode** to **Colour**.

- Leave the **Opacity** at **100%**.

2   On the Tools toolbar, click the ✎ **Paintbrush Tool**.

3   On the **Brush Tip** tab, in the **Basic** brush types list, you'll find soft and hard brushes, listed in that order. Choose an appropriate size soft brush tip. (We chose a 16 pixel brush.)

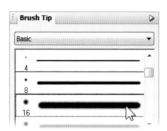

4   Use the 🔍 **Zoom Tool** to zoom into the area around one of the eyes.

5   On the **Colour** tab, set the foreground colour. (We chose **R=0, G=86, B=246**).

6   Start painting around the eye.

Don't worry about being too accurate with the paintbrush at this stage—the great advantage of painting on a layer is that you can delete any mistakes with the ✏️ **Standard Eraser**.

7   Repeat this procedure for the other eye.

Fine-tuning (optional)

If you've used the same colour as us, you'll notice it appears very bright. The great thing is that as we've painted onto a layer, we have several options to fine-tune the effect. We'll leave you with a few examples.

Option 1: Change the blend mode

1   On the **Layers** tab, select the 'Colour' layer.

2   In the blend mode drop-down list, click either **Overlay** or **Soft Light**. Notice the subtle change in the colour when using different blend mode types.

Examples

Overlay
blend mode
at 100% opacity

Soft Light
blend mode
at 100% opacity

Option 2: Reduce layer opacity

1   On the **Layers** tab, select the 'Colour' layer.

2   Click the arrow next to **Opacity** and drag the slider to the left to reduce the layer opacity. We found that 65% worked well.

Examples

Colour	**Overlay**	**Soft Light**
blend mode	blend mode	blend mode
at 65% opacity	at 65% opacity	at 65% opacity

That's it! Now that you know the basic principles, why not experiment with other photos and other colours? If you haven't done so already, you may also want to try the **Popping Colour** tutorial on p. 115.

Creating Infrared Effects

This tutorial aims to simulate the effect produced by infrared photography. Although humans can't see it, vegetation reflects a lot of infrared light (a wavelength between 760nm and 1000nm), which, when captured on an infrared film, appears very bright and vivid. Blue or bright sky also appears very dark as the blue light is filtered out. This produces a very interesting effect which we will demonstrate on an image of a tree.

By the end of this tutorial you will be able to:

- Use the **Screen** blend mode to increase brightness.

- Apply an effect to a single channel.

- Apply a **Channel Mixer** adjustment.

Go to **http://go.serif.com/resources/HPX4** to download the following tutorial project file(s):

○ **tree.jpg**

Let's begin...

- On the Standard toolbar, click 📂 **Open**.

- Locate the **tree.jpg** and click **Open**.

The infrared effect creates a 'glow' when the light is captured by a camera. We can simulate this effect very easily by applying a blur to a single channel. As infrared light reflects off green the most, this is the channel we'll apply the blend to. However, the first thing we need to do is increase the brightness. We can do this quickly using the **Screen** blend mode.

To apply a Screen blend mode:

1   On the **Layers** tab, right-click on the **Background** layer and click **Duplicate...**

2   In the **Duplicate Layer** dialog, click **OK**. The new layer is selected by default.

3   In the blend mode drop-down list, click **Screen**.

The image should now look completely over-exposed. Now we're ready to apply the blur to the green channel.

To apply an adjustment to a single channel:

1 On the **Channels** tab, click the **Green** channel.

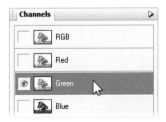

The green channel is displayed.

2 On the **Effects** menu, click **Blur > Gaussian Blur**.

3 In the dialog, set the **Radius** to approximately **5.0** and click **OK**.

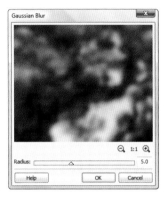

The blur is applied to the green channel.

4   On the **Channels** tab, click to select **RGB**. All channels are displayed again.

Our next step is to apply a **Channel Mixer** adjustment.

To apply a Channel Mixer adjustment:

1   On the **Adjustments** tab, click **Channel Mixer...** The Channel Mixer settings are displayed in the tab and a new adjustment layer is added to the **Layers** tab.

2   On the **Adjustments** tab:

•   Select the **Monochrome** option.

•   Change the **Red** channel to **100**.

•   Change the **Green** channel to **200**.

•   Change the **Blue** channel to **-200**.

- Change the **Constant** to **-61**.

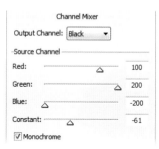

That's it! The infrared effect is complete!

Depth Maps

A depth map is an image that is laid on top of another image, a little like a stencil template. This relatively simple tutorial offers an interesting application for a depth map, with 3D Lighting control being used.

By the end of this tutorial you will be able to:

- Define, copy and paste selections.

- Apply a depth map.

- Apply **3D Depth** and **Lighting** effects.

To help you to complete the tutorial, we've provided our starting photo.

Go to **http://go.serif.com/resources/HPX4** to download the following tutorial project file(s):

- **beach.jpg**

You may also want the following depth maps to add to the photo:

- **DM01.jpg**
- **DM02.jpg**

Let's begin...

- On the Standard toolbar, click **Open**.

- Locate **beach.jpg** and click **Open**.

This image was chosen because it has a large amount of unspoiled sand. This makes it perfect for a depth map effect.

Layers

In the open image, notice that the **Layers** tab shows only one layer, 'Background'. You'll also see that several of the **Layer** tab options are greyed out. This is because a Background layer has different properties to a **standard** layer and doesn't support transparency.

Before we go any further, we need to convert the Background layer to a standard layer by **promoting** it.

To promote a layer:

1   On the **Layers** tab, right-click the Background layer and click **Promote to Layer**…

2   In the dialog, click **OK** to accept the default settings. The layer is renamed **Layer 1**. You'll see that all layer options are now available to you, including the options that we're going to use next.

🖎   The **Delete** button will only be available when you have more than one layer.

To add a Depth Map:

1   Click the  **Add Layer Depth Map** button, and then on the **Select** menu, click **Select All** (or press **Ctrl+A**) to create a selection around your image.

(You'll see a dotted line around the image indicating that it is selected.)

Now we'll open our depth map file.

2   Click **File**, then **Open**. Locate **DM01.jpg** and click **Open**.

3   On the **Select** menu, click **Select All** to select the whole image.

On the **Edit** menu, click **Copy** (or **Ctrl+C**) to copy the image to the Clipboard.

4   Close the **DM01.jpg** file. The original image is active again.

5   On the **Edit** menu, choose **Paste**, then **Into Selection** to paste the contents of your Clipboard into the selection.

Click **Select**, then **Deselect** (**Ctrl+D**) to deselect the image.

It doesn't look fantastic yet, but don't worry, there's more to come!

6   On the **Layers** tab, click **Add Layer Effects**.

7   In the **Layer Effects** dialog, notice that the **3D Effects** and **3D Lighting** check boxes are already selected.

•   Select **3D Effects** and set **Blur** to **2** and **Depth** to **9**.

•   Select **3D Lighting** and adjust the light source properties to your liking. We used **Angle 98** and **Elevation 46** and reduced the **Soften** setting to **3**.

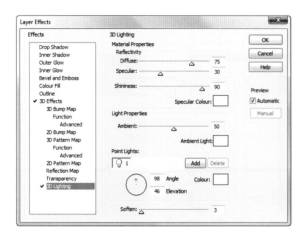

- Click **OK**.

Your image should resemble ours...

You can also create different effects by using the same starting image but by adding a different depth map. This image uses **DM02.jpg**.

Depth maps can be used to great effect with the right images. An image like this could make a great cover for a holiday album.

We're sure that you will have a lot of fun experimenting with this technique.

Introducing Weather Effects

Have you ever wished that you could control the weather? Well, now you can! In these advanced tutorials we'll be using some of the powerful tools in PhotoPlus X4 to create fantastic weather effects. If you haven't done so before, we recommend that you work through the earlier tutorials in this section as we'll be using many of the same techniques.

In these weather tutorials, we'll add a snow storm (p. 143) and make it rain (p. 167). Each tutorial starts from the same point that we've outlined in this introduction. We've also provided the images that you'll need for all of the tutorials in this set.

Go to **http://go.serif.com/resources/HPX4** to download the following tutorial project file(s):

pagoda.jpg

pagoda_template.png

By the end of this tutorial you will be able to:

* Add a selection template to an image as a separate layer.

Create a sunset or a phenomenal lightning storm by trying out our additional online tutorials at serif.com!

Let's begin...

1   On the Standard toolbar, click 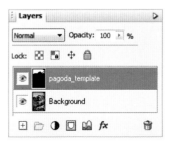 **Open**.

2   Locate the **pagoda.jpg** and click **Open**.

     Now, we need to open the template file as a new layer. It is easiest to do this by dragging the image from Windows Explorer.

3   In Windows, open an Explorer window and locate the **pagoda_template.png** file.

4   Click and drag the **pagoda_template.png** file into PhotoPlus and onto the existing image.

     The black and white template image opens as a new layer.

5   As we don't quite need the template just yet, click the button next to the **pagoda_template** layer to hide it.

The selection template

When creating weather effects, you will repeatedly need to select the same areas of the image. Our selection template is a simple black and white representation of the two most common selection areas. We created our initial selection and then on a separate layer, we filled part of the selection white and then filled the inverted selection black. The template was exported as an image file. Why not create one for your own images?

Don't forget to save your work!

Save your starting point as an SPP file, e.g., weather.spp. Then, make a copy of the file each time you want to start on the next weather effect so that you don't have to repeat these steps each time.

What now? Well, the next step is to choose the type of weather that you'd like to create next!

See each tutorial to get started: **Weather Effects: Snow** on p. 143 or **Weather Effects: Rain** on p. 167.

Weather Effects: Snow

Why go out in the cold winter weather to take a photo when all you need is a few minutes with PhotoPlus? In this advanced tutorial, we'll create a winter wonderland, complete with falling snow, around our Japanese pagoda image.

By the end of this tutorial you will be able to:

- Make a selection using the **Colour Range** dialog.

- Add and use layer masks and layer blend modes.

- Apply adjustment layers, noise and blur effects.

- For this tutorial, you will need to use the SPP file on p. 139. If you haven't done so already, you will also need to download the clouds.jpg.

Go to **http://go.serif.com/resources/HPX4** to download the following tutorial project file(s):

○ **clouds.jpg**

Let's begin...

- On the Standard toolbar, click 📂 **Open**.

- Browse to your saved copy of weather.spp file that you created in the **Introducing Weather Effects** tutorial and click **Open**.

  The project file opens in the workspace.

Toning down the colour

The colours in our starting image are very saturated. As a result, the first thing we need to do is to tone them down a little with a desaturation layer.

To create a desaturation layer:

1   On the **Layers** tab, click to select the 'Background' layer and then click ⊞ **New Layer**.

2   In the dialog, name the layer 'Desaturate' and click **OK**.

3   On the **Colour** tab, set the foreground colour to 50% grey (**RGB 128,128,128**).

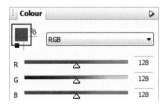

4   Click to select the ◆ **Flood Fill Tool** and then click inside the new layer to fill it.

5   On the **Layers** tab, change the blend mode to **Colour** and set **Opacity** to **30**%.

The colours in the image are subdued in a subtle way. Perfect!

 Don't forget to save your work!

Make it snow!

No winter image is complete without snow. Let's create that now. We can
create the initial effect by using a filter on a duplicate layer.

To create the snow layer:

1 On the **Layers** tab, right-click the 'Background' layer and click
   Duplicate...

2 For now, leave the default name, 'Background copy' and click **OK**.

3 Drag the new layer above the 'Desaturate' layer.

4 On the **Adjustments** tab, click **Black & White Film...**

   A new adjustment layer is added to the **Layers** tab.

5 On the **Adjustments** tab, set all of the colour values to **200**, apart from Cyan and Blue. (Leave these at the default setting.)

The image should resemble the illustration.

6 On the **Layers** tab, with the **Black and White Film** layer still selected, press and hold the **Shift** key and click the **Background Copy** layer to select it.

7 Right-click the selected layers and in the menu, click **Merge Selected Layers**.

The layers are merged into a single layer that takes its name from the top selected layer—in this case, **Black and White Film**.

8   Set the blend mode of the merged layer to **Screen**.

We now have an image that has areas of snow.

The next step exposes some of the original colour of the layer beneath. We can do this quickly with the **Colour Range** dialog.

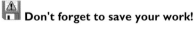 **Don't forget to save your work!**

To create a selection using the Colour Range dialog:

1   With the 'Black and White Film' layer selected, on the **Select** menu, click **Colour Range...**

2   In the dialog:

• Click the ✎ **Colour Picker** and ensure **Sampled Colours** is selected.

- Set the **Tolerance** slider to **70**.

- In the **Preview** drop-down menu, select **Overlay**.

- In the main window, click on a dark area of the image. It turns deep red to show that it is selected.

- Click **OK** to close the dialog.

The animated, dashed line outlines the selected areas.

3   Press the **Delete** key to permanently delete the selected area. Press **Ctrl+D** to deselect.

Although not immediately obvious, you should see some of the original colour, especially in the water. We'll add a mask to this layer to reveal the original sky colour...

4   Click to select and reveal the 'pagoda_template' layer.

5   On the **Select** menu, click **Colour Range...**

6 In the dialog:

- Click the  **Colour Picker** and ensure **Sampled Colours** is selected.

- Set the **Tolerance** slider to **95**.

- In the **Preview** drop-down menu, select **Overlay**.

- In the main window, click the white, sky area of the image. It turns deep red to show that it is selected.

- Click **OK** to close the dialog.

    The animated, dashed line shows the selection around the sky on the 'pagoda_template' layer.

7 On the **Layers** tab, click 👁 to hide the 'pagoda_template' layer and then select the **Black and White Film** layer. The selection remains in place.

8   On the **Layers** tab, press the **Alt** key and click  **Add Layer Mask** to apply a hide selection mask.

A mask is applied to the layer and the blue coloured sky is revealed.

The next step is to cool our sky down a few degrees. We'll do this by adjusting the **Colour Balance**. Your selection should still be in place. If not, repeat steps 4-7 of the previous section to select the sky.

To adjust the colour balance:

1   On the **Layers** tab, click the 'Background' layer to select it.

2   On the **Adjustments** tab, click **Colour Balance...**

A new adjustment layer is added to the **Layers** tab just above the 'Background' layer. Notice that a mask has been created for us from our selection.

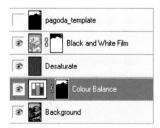

3   On the **Adjustments** tab:

- In **Tonal Balance** section, select **Midtones**.

- Make sure that the **Preserve Lightness** option is selected.

- In the **Colour Levels** section, insert the following values from left to right: **-69, 0, 68**.

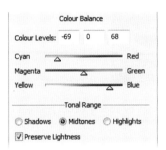

- Then, in the **Tonal Balance** section, select **Highlights**.

- In the **Colour Levels** section, enter the following values from left to right: **-32, 0, 22**.

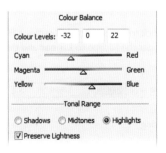

- The blue in the sky is increased.

Next we'll cool the whole image by adding a cool gradient layer.

To create a cool gradient:

1 On the **Layers** tab, select the **Black and White Film** layer and click ⊞ **New Layer**.

2 In the dialog, name the layer **Cool gradient** and click **OK**.

3 On the **Fill** flyout, click to select the ▭ **Gradient Fill Tool** and on the context toolbar, set the fill type to **Linear** and then click the colour sample.

4 In the **Gradient** dialog:

- Double-click the lower-left, black stop.

- In the **Adjust Colour** dialog select a light cyan colour. We used **RGB 205,250,250**.

- Click **OK** to return to the **Gradient** dialog.

- Double-click the lower-right, white stop.

- In the **Adjust Colour** dialog select a darker cyan colour. We used **RGB 147,238,250**.

- Click **OK** to return to the **Gradient** dialog.

5 The dialog shows a light to dark cyan gradient.

Click **OK** to exit.

6 With the **Cool gradient** layer still selected, click and drag a gradient line from the top of the image down to just past the bottom of the image. Release the mouse button to apply the gradient.

7 On the **Layers** tab, set the layer blend mode to **Colour** and reduce the **Opacity** to **35%**.

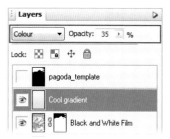

The image is really starting to shape up.

However, there is still 'snow' in all of the wrong places, such as beneath the roof of the building. Let's get the 'snow shovels' out and dig it up!

 Don't forget to save your work!

To erase unwanted 'snow':

1   On the Tools toolbar, click the ✏ **Paintbrush Tool** and on the **Brush Tip** tab, select the **Media - Charcoal** category and click to select brush **Grainy Smear**.

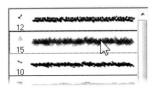

2   On the **Layers** tab, on the **Black and White Film** layer, click to select the mask thumbnail.

3   On the **Colour** tab, set the foreground colour to black.

4   Starting with the area below the roof, use the brush to gradually remove areas of snow from the building.

Also reveal some of the areas of land, water and trees amid the snow covering. You may need to adjust the brush size for different areas of the image. (We've also added a screenshot of our finished layer mask to help you with this stage.)

💡 When painting on the mask layer, you may find it helpful to zoom into the image and temporarily reduce the opacity of the 'Black and White Film' layer to see the original colours beneath.

The next step is to add a little depth to the image by creating some shaded areas in the snow.

To add shaded areas of snow:

1   On the **Layers** tab, select the **Black and White Film** layer and click ⊞ **New Layer**.

2   In the dialog, name the layer **Shaded snow** and click **OK**.

3   Set the layer blend mode to **Dodge**.

4   In the **Colour** tab, select a light, violet-blue colour. We used
    RGB 195,181,254.

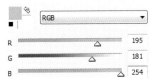

5   Set the ✏ **Paintbrush Tool** to **30**% opacity on the context
    toolbar, and paint the brush over some of the darker areas in the land
    and trees to give the impression of shaded snow. Don't forget that
    you can zoom in or out of your image at any time to work on
    different areas.

 Don't forget to save your work!

Replacing sky

Our image is almost complete but it's still missing something—falling snow.
However, we can't have snow without clouds. Let's add some to the sky
using a stock image.

To replace the sky:

1   On the **Layers** tab, select the 'Background' layer.

2   In Windows, open an Explorer window and locate the **clouds.jpg**
    file.

3 Click and drag the **clouds.jpg** file into PhotoPlus and onto the image.

The clouds image opens as a new layer.

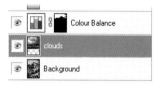

4 On the **Layers** tab, ensure that only the **clouds** layer is selected then, on the Tools toolbar, click the ▦ **Deform Tool**.

5 Drag the handles inwards to resize the clouds layer to the same width as the rest of the image.

6 Select the 'pagoda_template' layer. On the **Select** menu click **Colour Range...** In the dialog, select the sky region and click **OK**. (See steps 4-7 in 'To create a selection using the Colour Range dialog:' on p. 148 if you need a reminder of how to do this).

7 On the **Layers** tab, click to select the **clouds** layer and then click ▣ **Add Layer Mask**.

The selection is revealed and the unwanted area of cloud is hidden by the mask.

8 Press **Ctrl+D** to deselect the sky area.

9 On the **Layers** tab, set the blend mode of the 'clouds' layer to **Screen**.

Don't forget to save your work!

Creating a snow storm

Now that the clouds are in place we can add our finishing touch, falling snow.

To create the falling snow:

1   On the **Layers** tab, click to select the **Cool gradient** layer and then click ⊞ **New Layer**.

2   In the dialog, rename the layer 'Falling snow' and click **OK**.

3   On the Tools toolbar, click the ◈ **Flood Fill Tool** and on the **Colour** tab, set the foreground colour to 50% grey, **RGB 128,128,128**.

4   Click on the layer to fill it—your layer should be flat grey.

5   On the **Layers** tab, right-click on the 'Falling snow' layer and click **Convert to Filter Layer**.

6   On the **Effects** menu, click **Noise > Add Noise...** In the dialog, set the **Percentage** to **100** and the **Distribution** to **Gaussian**. Click **OK**.

7   On the **Effects** menu, click **Blur > Gaussian Blur...**

8   In the dialog, set the **Radius** to **2.0**. Click **OK**.

Your layer won't look much like snow. However, the next few steps will see that change...

9   On the **Image** menu, click **Adjust > Levels...**

10 In the **Levels** dialog:

- Set the first input (black point) value to **145**.

- Set the second input (white point) value to **159**.

- Set the **Gamma** to **1.00**.

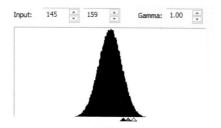

- Click **OK**.

11 On the **Effects** menu, click **Blur > Motion Blur...**

12 In the dialog, set the **Distance** to **5** and set the **Angle** to **230**. Click **OK**.

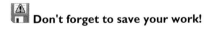

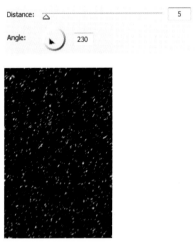

13 On the **Layers** tab, set the **Falling snow** layer blend mode to **Screen**.

⚠️ **Don't forget to save your work!**

That's it! A beautiful winter scene complete with falling snow!

Weather Effects: Rain

In this tutorial we're going to quite literally make it rain. Don't worry, there is strictly no singing or dancing involved, only the powerful tools in PhotoPlus.

By the end of this tutorial you will be able to:

- Replace the sky with another image.

- Make a selection using the **Colour Range** dialog.

- Add and use layer masks and blend modes.

- Create a custom gradient and apply noise and blur effects.

⚠ For this tutorial, you'll need to use the SPP file created on p. 139. If you haven't done so already, you will also need to download the clouds.jpg file.

🔵 Go to **http://go.serif.com/resources/HPX4** to download the following tutorial project file(s):

🔵 **clouds.jpg**

Let's begin...

- On the Standard toolbar, click  **Open**.

- Browse to your saved copy of weather.spp file that you created in the **Introducing Weather Effects** tutorial and click **Open**.

  The project file opens in the workspace.

Replacing a sky

Now we're ready to get down to the business of creating some weather! Rain comes with rain clouds. Unfortunately, our image has a brilliant, blue sky; however, we can easily fix this! Let's begin by replacing the sky with the **clouds.jpg** image.

To replace the sky:

1 On the **Layers** tab, select the 'Background' layer.

2 In Windows, open an Explorer window and locate the **clouds.jpg** file.

3 Click and drag the **clouds.jpg** file into PhotoPlus and onto the image.

  The clouds image opens as a new layer.

4 On the **Layers** tab, ensure that only the **clouds** layer is selected then, on the Tools toolbar, click the **Deform Tool**.

5   Drag the handles inwards to resize the clouds layer to the same width as the rest of the image. (Press **Shift** while dragging to maintain the aspect ratio.)

6   Select the 'pagoda_template' layer. On the **Select** menu, click **Colour Range...**

7   In the dialog:

  •   Click the ⚲ **Colour Picker** and ensure **Sampled Colours** is selected.

  •   Set the **Tolerance** slider to **95**.

  •   In the **Preview** drop-down menu, select **Overlay**.

- In the main window, click the white, sky area of the image. It turns deep red to show that it is selected.

- Click **OK** to close the dialog.

8   On the **Layers** tab, click to select the 'clouds' layer and then click ▣ **Add Layer Mask**.

The selection is revealed and the unwanted area of cloud is hidden by the mask.

9   Press **Ctrl+D** to deselect the sky area.

10   On the **Layers** tab, set the blend mode of the **clouds** layer to **Lightness**.

Don't forget to save your work!

Toning down the colour

Our image is very bright with saturated colours. For the rain effect to be convincing, we need to tone the colours down a little. As in previous tutorials, we can create a desaturation layer.

To create a desaturation layer:

1   On the **Layers** tab, ensure the 'clouds' layer is selected and then click ⊞ **New Layer**.

2   In the dialog, name the layer 'Desaturate' and click **OK**.

3   On the **Colour** tab, set the foreground colour to 50% grey (**RGB 128,128,128**).

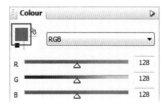

4   Click to select the ◈ **Flood Fill Tool** and then click inside the new layer to fill it.

5   On the **Layers** tab, change the blend mode to **Colour** and set **Opacity** to **40%**.

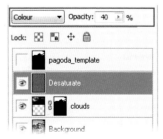

The colours in the image are looking much more suitable.

 Don't forget to save your work!

Getting darker

The next step is to darken parts of the image to create a gloomier feel.

To darken the image:

1   On the **Layers** tab, make sure that the **Desaturate** layer is selected and then click ⊞ **New Layer**. In the dialog, name the layer **Darken** and click **OK**.

2   On the Tools toolbar, click the ◈ **Flood Fill Tool**.

3   On the **Colour** tab, set the foreground colour to a dark blue. We used **RGB 47,0,101**.

4   Click on the image to fill the layer.

Finally, on the **Layers** tab, set the blend mode to **Darken** and reduce the **Opacity** to **70%**.

The sky is about the right colour but the rest of the image is too dark.

We can correct this by using another mask.

5   Select the 'pagoda_template layer' and on the **Select** menu, click **Colour Range...** Select the sky area as in step 7 of the **To replace the sky** section (p. 168) and click **OK** to close the dialog.

6   On the **Layers** tab, click 👁 to hide the 'pagoda_template' layer and then select the **Darken** layer.

7   Click ▢ **Add Layer Mask**.

The sky is still the correct colour, but the mask has removed all of the darkening effect from the rest of the image. Ideally, we need something that is half way between.

To create a part opacity mask:

So far, we have only used black and white masks. Let's show you what happens if we use another colour.

1   On the **Layers** tab, press the **Alt** key and click the mask thumbnail. The black and white mask is displayed and your sky selection should still be in place.

2   On the **Select** menu, click **Invert** to invert the selection.

3 On the **Colour** tab, set the foreground colour to 50% grey (**L 128**).

4 On the Tools toolbar, click the ◈ **Flood Fill Tool** and click within the selection to fill it grey.

5 On the **Layers** tab, click once on the blue layer thumbnail to hide the mask again.

The image is already looking better, but we could give the impression that the sun is attempting to break through the cloud by adding more of the original colour to the building.

6   On the 'Darken' layer, click the mask thumbnail to select it.

7   On the **Colour** tab, set the foreground colour to black and on the Tools toolbar, click the ✎ **Paintbrush Tool**.

8   On **Brush Tip** tab, choose a soft, round brush and on the context toolbar, set the brush **Opacity** to around **75%**.

9   With the selection still in place, carefully paint over the building, the top of the tree line and the foreground rocks to bring back some colour. The selection prevents the brush strokes from spilling over into the sky. Notice that the thumbnail updates accordingly.

10   When you are happy with the amount of colour in the image, press **Ctrl+D** to remove the selection.

⚠️ **Don't forget to save your work!**

Over the rainbow...

Sun and rain often create a rainbow. Let's add one now using a custom created gradient.

To create the rainbow:

1   On the **Layers** tab, ensure that the **Darken** layer is selected and click ⊞ **New Layer**.

2   In the dialog, name the layer 'Rainbow' and click **OK**.

3   On the Fill flyout, click to select the ▢ **Gradient Fill Tool** and on the context toolbar, set the fill type to **Radial** and then click the colour sample.

4   In the **Gradient** dialog:

   •   Click the rainbow-like gradient.

   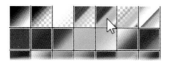

   •   Click between the yellow and red stops to automatically add an orange colour stop.

- Working from the lower-left, click to select the red stop and then click **Delete**.

- Double-click the pink stop to open the **Adjust Colour** dialog. Select the purple swatch (**RGB 193,0,193**) and click **OK**.

- Click to select the orange stop and set the **Location** to **89**%. Starting with the stops nearest the orange, drag each stop so that it is virtually touching the one next to it as illustrated.

- Set the **Smoothness** to **0**%.

- Next, click to select the upper-left opacity stop and set the **Location** to **67**%. Set the upper-right opacity stop **Location** to **97**%.

- Click in between the two opacity stops to add another opacity stop.

- Finally, set the **Opacity** of the middle opacity stop to 75% and set the left and right opacity stops to **0% Opacity**. The gradient properties should look approximately like the illustration.

5   Click **OK** to exit the **Gradient** dialog.

The 'Rainbow' layer should still be selected.

💡 Before you continue, why not save your gradient? Open the **Gradient** dialog again and right-click in the gradient swatch panel. Click **Add Item**. Your new swatch is added to the Default gradient category.

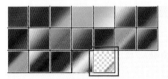

6   Click on the workspace outside your image and drag a gradient line from right to left.

(If you can't see the workspace you may need to zoom out a little.) Release the mouse button to apply the gradient.

7   On the Tools toolbar, click the **Move Tool**.

8   Drag the rainbow into position so that it curves around the building towards the water.

9   On the **Layers** tab, right-click the 'Rainbow' layer and click **Convert to Filter Layer...**

10   On the **Effects** menu, click **Blur > Gaussian Blur...**

11   In the dialog:

    •   Set the **Radius** to **20**.

    •   Click **OK**.

12   On the **Layers** tab, reduce the **Opacity** of the 'Rainbow' layer to **80**%.

The gradient looks much more rainbow-like.

The next step is to remove the unwanted part of the curve. How? With a mask of course!

 Don't forget to save your work!

To mask the rainbow:

1   On the **Layers** tab, click ⊞ **Add Layer Mask**.

2   On the Tools toolbar, click the ▭ **Gradient Fill Tool**.

3   On the context toolbar, set the gradient type to **Linear** then, click the colour sample to open the **Gradient** dialog.

4   In the dialog, click to select the black to white gradient and then click **OK** to exit.

5 Ensure that the **Rainbow** layer mask thumbnail is selected and then, click and drag a gradient line from just below centre of the image to the top.

Release the mouse button to apply the gradient.

Notice that the rainbow now fades as it gets closer to the water.

Perfect. However, there's something missing. We need a reflection.

To create the reflection:

1   Right-click the 'Rainbow' layer and click **Duplicate...**

2   On the **Image** menu, click **Flip Vertically > Layer**.

3   On the Tools toolbar, click the ⊹ **Move Tool**.

4   Drag the reflected image down so that it mirrors the 'Rainbow' layer.

5   On the **Layers** tab, click to select the 'Rainbow copy' mask thumbnail.

6   On the **Colour** tab, click ▪ reset the foreground colour to black and then click the ✏ **Paintbrush Tool**.

7   Paint over the rocks with a soft, round brush set to **100% Opacity** to remove the unwanted reflection.

8   Finally, reduce the layer **Opacity** to **35%**.

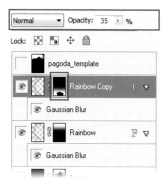

Our work is almost complete.

Don't forget to save your work!

Creating the rain

We have one more effect to add. Let's make it rain!

To create the rain:

1   On the **Layers** tab, ensure that the 'Rainbow copy' layer is selected
    and click ⊞ **New Layer**. In the dialog, rename the layer **Rain** and
    click **OK**.

2   On the Tools toolbar, on the Fill flyout, click the ◆ **Flood Fill Tool**
    and on the **Colour** tab, set the foreground colour to **RGB
    128,128,128**. Click on the layer to fill it.

3   On the **Layers** tab, right-click on the 'Falling snow' layer and click
    Convert to Filter Layer.

4   On the **Effects** menu, click **Noise > Add Noise...**

5   In the dialog, set the **Percentage** to **90** and the **Distribution** to
    Uniform. Click **OK**.

6   On the **Image** menu, click **Adjust > Levels...**

7   In the **Levels** dialog set the first input (black point) value to **110** and click **OK**.

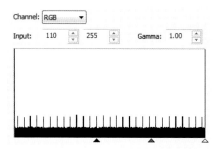

8   On the **Effects** menu, click **Blur > Gaussian Blur...** and in the dialog, set the **Radius** to **0.5** and click **OK**.

9   Next, on the **Effects** menu, click **Blur > Motion Blur...** and in the dialog, set the **Distance** to **25** and the **Angle** to **60**. Click **OK**.

10 Once again, we need a final effect. On the **Effects** menu, click **Other > High Pass...** and in the dialog, set the **Radius** to **70**. Click **OK**.

11 Finally, on the **Layers** tab, set the **Rain** layer blend mode to **Hard Light**.

Congratulations! You've made it rain!

Hopefully you'll have enjoyed this tutorial and you'll have learnt to use some powerful tools and techniques in the process. All you need to do now is experiment with other images. Have fun and good luck!

Makeover Studio

In this set of tutorials, we'll focus our attention on digital makeover techniques.

Whether you want to remove red eye, remove under-eye dark circles, whiten teeth, smooth out skin, or erase a blemish, these retouching tricks will enhance any portrait photo.

(Whether or not you choose to let your subject in on the secret is up to you!).

Removing Red Eye

Red eye is caused when light from the flash of a camera reflects off the back of a subject's eye the instant a photograph is taken. If your photos suffer from this, don't worry—it's simple to correct in PhotoPlus!

By the end of this tutorial you will be able to:

- Add a duplicate layer for non-destructive amendments.

- Use the **Red Eye Tool** to correct red eye effects.

You can apply this correction on a duplicate layer (recommended), or directly to your image.

Let's begin...

1   On the Standard toolbar, click 📂 **Open**.

2   Locate your chosen photo and click **Open**.

    The image opens in the workspace

To remove red eye:

1   On the **Layers** tab, right-click the layer containing your image and
    then click **Duplicate**. In the **Duplicate Layer** dialog, name your
    layer and click **OK**.

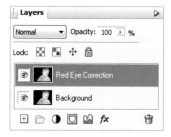

2   On the Standard toolbar, click the 🔍 **Zoom Tool** and then click to
    zoom in on the subject's pupil.

3   On the Retouch Tools flyout, click the 👁 **Red Eye Tool**.

4   Click once on the eye to set a default red eye correct size.

     - or -

     Click and drag to draw an ellipse around the red area and then
     release the mouse button.

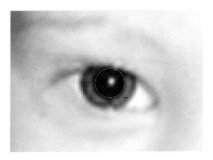

⚠   Don't make the ellipse too large as you may affect other
      red-based areas of the photo.

Removing Blemishes

Remove spots and blemishes to leave skin looking superb!

PhotoPlus provides several tools for removing skin blemishes and flaws. All of the following techniques can be applied directly to an image, but for best practice, we'll use duplicate layers for methods 1 and 2, and a transparent layer for method 3.

By the end of this tutorial you will be able to:

- Add a duplicate layer for non-destructive amendments.

- Use the **Blemish Remover Tool** to quickly remove small blemishes.

- Use the **Patch Tool** to blend away larger areas of blemished skin.

- Use the **Clone Tool** to carefully remove spots using areas of unblemished skin.

Method 1: Blemish Remover

Use the 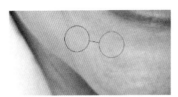 **Blemish Remover** to remove small skin blemishes and other flaws.

1   On the **Layers** tab, right-click the layer containing your image and then click **Duplicate**. In the **Duplicate Layer** dialog, name your layer and click **OK**.

2   On the Tools toolbar, on the Blemish Tools flyout, select the **Blemish Remover**.

3   On the context toolbar, set your **Blemish Remover** tip size—this will depend on the region under repair.

4   Click on the blemish to define the target area.

5   Drag to select a suitable pickup area to replace the blemish (the outlined target area updates as you drag), then release the mouse button to apply the correction.

Method 2: Patch Tool

Use the 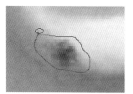 **Patch Tool** to remove irregular shaped blemishes and flaws.

1   On the **Layers** tab, right-click the layer containing your image and then click **Duplicate**. In the **Duplicate Layer** dialog, name your layer and click **OK**.

2   On the Standard toolbar, click the 🔍 **Zoom Tool** and then click on your image to zoom into the area you want to work on.

3   On the Tools toolbar, on the Blemish Tools flyout, select the ◈ **Patch Tool**.

4   Click and drag on your image to outline the area you want to remove.

5   Drag the selected area over to a suitable pickup area to replace the blemish. The outlined target area updates as you drag.

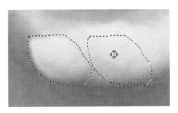

6   Release the mouse button to apply the correction. Repeat as required.

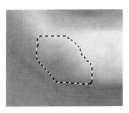

7   To adjust the effect, drag the **Opacity** slider on the **Layers** tab.

Method 3: Clone Tool

Use the ♨ **Clone Tool** to cover flaws, or remove unwanted areas, by copying a selection from one area to another.

1   On the **Layers** tab, click ⊞ **New Layer**. In the **Layer Properties** dialog, name your layer and click **OK**. PhotoPlus adds a new transparent layer to the **Layers** tab.

2   On the Tools toolbar, on the Clone Tools flyout, click the ♨ **Clone Tool**.

3 On the **Brush Tip** tab, choose a brush tip (generally soft-tipped is best, but this will depend on your image).

4 On the context toolbar, set your brush tip **Size**—this will depend on the region under repair, and select the **Use all layers** check box.

5 Press and hold down the **Shift** key and then click to define a pickup point.

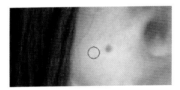

6 Hold down the mouse button and brush on the image to lay down paint (the cross-hair indicates the region being copied).

Release the mouse button to end the stroke.

Removing Dark Circles

There are several techniques you can use to remove under-eye dark circles. We'll explore these techniques in this tutorial, but you should choose the technique you find most effective for your photo.

By the end of this tutorial you will be able to:

- Add a duplicate layer for non-destructive amendments.

- Use the **Colour Pickup** and **Paintbrush Tools** to give a smooth, airbrushed effect.

- Use **Curves adjustment** for subtle results.

- Use the **Patch Tool** to replace dark circles with a selected lighter area.

- Adjust **Blend Mode** and **Opacity** on a layer.

Method 1: Paintbrush

Use the ✏ **Paintbrush** to paint out dark circles. We'll use a duplicate layer for this technique.

1   On the **Layers** tab, right-click the layer containing your image and then click **Duplicate.** In the **Duplicate Layer** dialog, name your layer and click **OK**.

2   On the Standard toolbar, click the 🔍 **Zoom Tool** and then click on your image to zoom into the eye area.

3   On the Tools toolbar, click the ✏ **Colour Pickup Tool**.

4   On the context toolbar, in the drop-down list, select **3 x 3 Average**.

5   Click on a suitable area of the skin to use as a colour to paint over the dark circles.

Over on the **Colour** tab, the **Foreground** colour swatch updates with the new pickup colour.

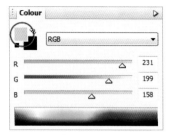

6   On the Tools toolbar, click the 🖌 **Paintbrush**.

7   On the context toolbar, set the blend mode to **Lightness** and the **Opacity** to 20%.

On the **Brush Tip** tab, select a small soft brush tip and then brush over the dark circles to lighten them.

Method 2: Curves adjustment

Use a **Curves adjustment** to minimize dark circles by adjusting tonal balance. We'll use an adjustment layer and a layer mask for this photo correction.

1   On the **Adjustments** tab, click **Curves...**.

2   A Curves adjustment layer and a **Reveal All** mask (filled with white) are added to the **Layers** tab.

The mask is automatically selected on the **Curves** adjustment layer; the mask thumbnail next to the layers name has a white border.

3 On the **Adjustments** tab, drag the centre of the diagonal line up, to form a gentle curve. (As you do this, you'll see your image lighten slightly.)

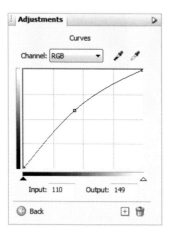

4 On the **Image** menu, click **Adjust** and then select **Negative Image**.

5 On the Tools toolbar, click the ✎ **Paintbrush**, then on the context toolbar, set the tool's blend mode to **Normal** and the **Opacity** to 100%.

6   On the **Colour** tab, set the foreground colour to white.

7   On the **Brush Tip** tab or context toolbar, select a small soft brush tip and then brush over the dark circles.

To adjust the effect, on the **Layers** tab, drag the layer **Opacity** slider.

Method 3: Patch tool

Use the ⬤ **Patch Tool** to replace dark circles with a lighter area of skin. We will make this correction on a duplicate layer.

1   On the **Layers** tab, right-click the layer containing your image and then click **Duplicate**.

2   In the **Duplicate Layer** dialog, name your layer and click **OK**.

3   On the Standard toolbar, click the 🔍 **Zoom Tool** and then click on your image to zoom into the eye area.

4   On the Tools toolbar, on the Blemish Tools flyout, click the ⬤ **Patch Tool**.

5   Click and drag on your image to outline the area you want to remove.

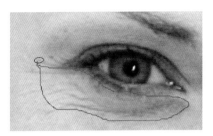

6   Drag the selected area over to a suitable pickup area to replace the blemish.

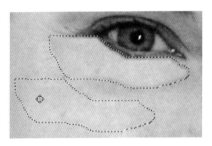

7   Release the mouse button to apply the correction. To adjust the effect, on the **Layers** tab, drag the layer **Opacity** slider.

Smoothing Skin

In this tutorial, we present you with several techniques to create smoother, softer looking skin, including converting a standard photo into a glamour portrait. There are subtle modifications you can make or more radical procedures. The technique you choose depends on your subject matter and the overall effect you want to achieve.

By the end of this tutorial you will be able to:

- Add a duplicate layer for non-destructive amendments.

- Convert a standard layer to a filter layer and use a filter from the **Filter Gallery**.

- Add a mask to your selected layer.

- Adjust the **Opacity** on a layer.

- Use the **Scratch Remover Tool** for subtle effects.

- Use the **Patch Tool** for larger areas.

Method 1: Gaussian Blur and Paintbrush 1

Blurs and softens facial lines and other flaws without affecting the rest of the image. This technique can produce subtle or dramatic results.

1   On the **Layers** tab, right-click the layer containing your image and then click **Duplicate**. In the **Duplicate Layer** dialog, name your layer and click **OK**.

2   Right-click the duplicate layer and then click **Convert to Filter Layer**.

3   From the Photo Studio toolbar, click 🔲 **Filter Gallery**.

    In the gallery, expand the **Blur** category and click the **Gaussian** swatch. Set the **Radius** to **6** and click **OK**. The radius size may have to be adjusted with image size.

The effect is added as part of a filter group on the filter layer, and applied to the image.

4   Right-click the filter group and select **Add Mask>Hide All**.

5   On the **Layers** tab, set the layer **Opacity** to **50%** and ensure the mask thumbnail is selected.

6   On the Standard toolbar, click the 🔍 **Zoom Tool** and click on your image to zoom into the area to be smoothed.

7   On the Tools toolbar, click the ✏ **Paintbrush**.

8   On the **Colour** tab, set the **Foreground** colour swatch to white.

9   Select a small soft brush tip, and then brush over the skin to smooth it.

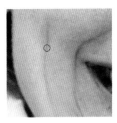

🖎   **To increase or decrease smoothing:**

On the **Layers** tab, adjust the filter layer's **Opacity**.

- or -

Double-click the **Gaussian** blur effect and then adjust the **Radius** setting.

Method 2: Scratch Remover

This method blends and softens discrete areas of the image only—laughter lines, frown lines, and so on—without affecting the rest of the image. This technique is great when you want subtle results.

1   On the **Layers** tab, right-click the layer containing your image and then click **Duplicate**. In the **Duplicate Layer** dialog, name your layer and click **OK**.

2   On the **Layers** tab, select the duplicate layer and set the layer **Opacity** to **50%**.

3   On the Standard toolbar, click the 🔍 **Zoom Tool**. Click on your image to zoom into the area to be smoothed.

4   On the Blemish Tools flyout, click the 🗡 **Scratch Remover**.

5   On the context toolbar, select **Use all layers**.

6   On the **Brush Tip** tab, choose a small soft brush tip.

7   Press and hold down the **Shift** key and then click to define a pickup point.

8   Click on the image to smooth skin.

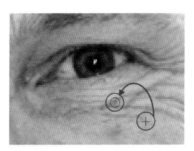

You'll get better results if you lay down paint using single clicks, rather than by clicking and dragging.

Smoothing Skin

Method 3: Gaussian Blur and Paintbrush 2

This method gives all areas of skin a smooth silky feel, while keeping facial details (eyes, lips, teeth, and so on) sharp. This technique is particularly suited to portrait and glamour shots.

1   On the **Layers** tab, right-click the layer containing your image and then click **Duplicate**. In the **Duplicate Layer** dialog, name your layer and click **OK**.

2   Right-click the duplicate layer and then click **Convert to Filter Layer**.

3   From the Photo Studio toolbar, click 🖰 **Filter Gallery**.

    In the gallery, expand the **Blur** category and click the **Gaussian** swatch. Set the **Radius** to **5** and click **OK**. The radius size may have to be adjusted with image size.

4   On the **Layers** tab, right-click the selected filter group (nested under the filter layer) and select **Add Mask>Reveal All**.

5   Set the layer **Opacity** to **50%** and ensure the mask thumbnail is selected.

6   On the Standard toolbar, click the 🔍 **Zoom** tool. Click on your image to zoom into the area where you want to restore detail.

7   On the Tools toolbar, click the 🖌 **Paintbrush**.

8   On the **Colour** tab, set the **Foreground** colour swatch to black.

9   Select a small soft brush tip, and then paint over the facial details you want to sharpen.

Method 4: Patch Tool

This method replaces wrinkles with a selected area of smoother skin.

1   On the **Layers** tab, right-click the layer containing your image and then click **Duplicate**. In the **Duplicate Layer** dialog, name your layer and click **OK**.

2   Click the 🔍 **Zoom Tool**, and then click on the area to be worked on.

3   On the Blemish Tools flyout, click the 🔷 **Patch Tool**.

4   Click and drag on your image to outline the area you want to smooth.

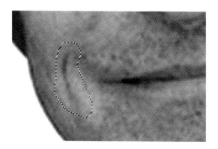

5   Drag the selected area over to a suitable pickup area to replace the blemish (the outlined target area updates as you drag), then release the mouse button to apply the correction.

6   To increase or reduce the effect, adjust the layer **opacity**.

Adding Sparkle

In this tutorial, we present you with a simple method to add sparkle to your subject's eyes and bring your portrait photos to life.

By the end of this tutorial you will be able to:

- Add a duplicate layer for non-destructive amendments.

- Convert a standard layer to a filter layer and use a filter from the **Filter Gallery**.

- Add a mask to your selected layer.

- Use the **Paintbrush Tool**.

To add sparkle:

1   On the **Layers** tab, right-click the layer containing your image and then click **Duplicate**. In the **Duplicate Layer** dialog, name your layer and click **OK**.

2   Right-click the duplicate layer and then click **Convert to Filter Layer**.

3   From the Photo Studio toolbar, click 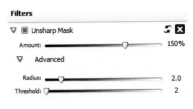 **Filter Gallery**.

In the **Filter Gallery**, expand the **Sharpen** category and click the **Unsharp Mask** swatch.

Expand the Advanced settings and adjust the effect by dragging the **Amount**, **Radius**, and **Threshold** sliders, or by typing values directly into the value boxes. Enter the following values:

- **Amount** 150%

- **Radius** 2.0

- **Threshold** 2

Click **OK**.

4   On the **Layers** tab, right-click the selected filter group (nested under the filter layer) and select **Add Mask>Hide All**.

5   On the Standard toolbar, click the 🔍 **Zoom** tool and click on your image to zoom into the eye area.

6 On the Tools toolbar, click the ✎ **Paintbrush**.

7 On the **Colour** tab, set the foreground colour to white.

8 On the **Brush Tip** tab, select a small soft brush tip.

9 Paint over the eyes to sharpen.

10 To adjust the effect, on the **Layers** tab, adjust the filter layer's **Opacity**.

- or -

Double-click the Unsharp Mask effect and then adjust its settings.

💡 For the ultimate in eye enhancement, combine this technique with the whitening method (see p. 231).

Removing Hotspots

In this tutorial, we show you a quick, easy technique to reduce hotspots and glare caused by uneven lighting or your camera's flash. This subtle makeover can dramatically transform your portrait photos.

By the end of this tutorial you will be able to:

- Add a duplicate layer for non-destructive amendments.

- Use the **Clone Tool** to tone down or hide hotspots.

- Adjust **Blend Mode** and **Opacity** on a layer.

To remove hotspots:

1   On the **Layers** tab, right-click the layer containing the image you want to work on and click **Duplicate**. In the **Duplicate Layer** dialog, name your layer and click **OK**.

2   On the **Layers** tab, select the duplicate layer.

3   On the Tools toolbar, from the Clone Tools flyout, click the ⚗ **Clone Tool**.

4   On the context toolbar, set the blend mode to **Darken**; set the **Opacity** to **50**%; and select the **Use all layers** check box.

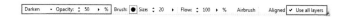

5   On the **Brush Tip** tab, select a large soft brush tip.

6   Hold down the **Shift** key and then click once in an area of skin with no hotspots.

7   Brush over the hotspots to fade them.

Slimming

Use this quick and easy technique to slim the subject of your photo.

By the end of this tutorial you will be able to:

- Use the **Deform Tool** to quickly trim a few pounds from your subject.

To digitally slim a subject:

1   On the **Layers** tab, select the layer containing your image.

2   On the Tools toolbar, click the  **Deform Tool**.

3   A rectangular bounding box, with sizing handles displays around the image.

4   Drag one of the side handles horizontally towards the centre of the image.

5   The further you drag, the slimmer the subject becomes.

   Generally a reduction of about 5% works well without looking fake.

Faking a Tan

Enhance your portrait photos and give your subjects a healthy glow by applying a fake suntan (subtle or strong).

By the end of this tutorial you will be able to:

- Add a new layer and adjust its **Blend Mode** and **Opacity**.

- Use the **Flood Fill Tool** and **Colour Tab**.

- Add a **mask** to a layer.

- Use the **Paintbrush Tool** and adjust its **Opacity**.

To fake a tan:

1   On the **Layers** tab, click ⊞ **New Layer**. In the **Layer Properties** dialog, name your layer and click **OK**. PhotoPlus adds a new transparent layer to the **Layers** tab.

2   On the **Layers** tab, select the new layer. Set the blend mode to **Soft Light** and the **Opacity** to **50%**.

3   On the Tools toolbar, click the ✎ **Flood Fill Tool**.

4   On the **Colour** tab, set the foreground colour to brown (we used RGB 110, 80, 41).

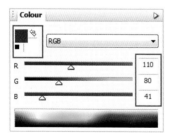

5   Click on the image to apply a brown fill to the layer.

6   On the **Layers** menu, select **Mask>Add Mask>Hide All**.

7 On the **Layers** tab, ensure the mask is selected.

8 Click the 🔍 **Zoom Tool** and click on the image to zoom into the area to be worked on first.

9 Click the ✏ **Paintbrush**. On the context toolbar, set the blend mode to **Normal** and the **Opacity** to **75%**.

10 On the **Colour** tab, set the foreground colour to white.

11 Select a soft brush tip, and then paint over the skin.

Adjust the layer opacity to reduce or increase the depth of the suntan.

Whitening Teeth and Eyes

Use this simple technique to give teeth a natural-looking sparkle and brighten the whites of eyes.

By the end of this tutorial you will be able to:

- Add a duplicate layer for non-destructive amendments.

- Use the **Dodge Tool** to quickly whiten a smile and brighten eyes.

🖎 If you are applying multiple **Makeover Studio** techniques, apply this one last.

To whiten teeth:

1   On the **Layers** tab, right-click the layer containing your image and then click **Duplicate**. In the **Duplicate Layer** dialog, name your layer and click **OK**.

2   On the **Layers** tab, select the duplicate layer and set the layer **Opacity** to **50%**.

3   On the Standard toolbar, click the 🔍 **Zoom Tool** and then click on your image to zoom into the mouth or eye area.

4   On the Retouch Tools flyout, click the 🔍 **Dodge Tool**.

5   On the context toolbar, in the **Tones** drop-down list, select **Midtones**.

6   On the **Brush Tip** tab, in the **Basic** category, you'll find a range of soft and hard brushes, listed in that order, in sizes from 1 to 256 pixels. Select a small soft brush tip.

7   Click and drag over the teeth, or the whites of the eyes, to brighten
them.

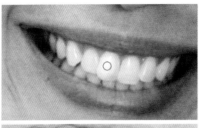

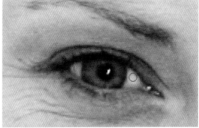

🖎   To reduce or increase the whitening effect, adjust the
layer opacity.

💡   For the ultimate in eye enhancement, combine this
technique with the sparkling method (see p. 220).

Macros

A macro is a saved sequence of steps (commands, keyboard strokes, mouse clicks, and so on) that can be stored and then recalled later with a single command or keyboard stroke.

Macros are particularly useful for storing multi-step tasks that are carried out repeatedly, or complex procedures that are time-consuming to reproduce.

In addition to allowing you to create your own macros (see the **Macros and Batch Processing** tutorial), PhotoPlus provides an extensive selection of predefined macros. With these, you can quickly and easily enhance, manipulate, and apply creative effects to your images.

Macros

On the **Macros** tab, in the drop-down list, the following predefined macro categories are available for selection:

- Black & White Photography
- Colour
- Commands
- Effects
- Frames
- Gradient Maps
- Layout Blurs
- New Document Landscape (print)*
- New Document Landscape (screen)*
- New Document Portrait (print)*
- New Document Portrait (screen)*
- Photography
- Selection
- Text Effects
- Text Outlines
- Textures
- Vignettes

These macros are not documented in this Resource Guide.

To see the various steps associated with a macro, click the arrow to the left of the macro name. The check boxes allow you to disable and enable each step. Some macros—for example, Effects/Pen Sketch—let you choose to open a relevant dialog to allow customization of the macro settings.

For more information on macro settings, see the *PhotoPlus User Guide* or *PhotoPlus Help*.

Black & White Photography

The **Black & White Photography** macros allow you to apply filter effects and techniques used in this style of photography.

You could apply the **Infrared (Dreamy)** option to make your image look like a fine art print, or you could apply the **Greyscale** option to create a documentary feel.

Original   Infrared (Dreamy)   Greyscale

Colour Filters

Colour filters in the **Black & White Photography** category allow you to convert an image to black and white, while also correcting or emphasizing the colours in the original image.

Red Filter   Yellow Filter   Green Filter   Orange Filter   Blue Filter

Apply Red Filter   Apply Yellow Filter   Apply Green Filter   Apply Orange Filter   Apply Blue Filter

Colour

The **Colour** macros allow you to apply a 'colour wash' effect to an image. For example, you might want to create a particular mood—try the **Recolour Blue** option; instantly 'age' your photo—**Recolour Sepia**; or simply recolour an image to suit a particular colour scheme.

Original

Greyscale	Recolour Red	Recolour Blue	Recolour Green
Image converted to greyscale	Image coloured red using Hue/Saturation/ Lightness	Image coloured blue	Image coloured green

Recolour Orange	Recolour Yellow	Recolour Sepia	Recolour Pink
Image coloured orange	Image coloured yellow	Image coloured sepia	Image coloured pink

Recolour Purple	Recolour (options)	Quad Colour	Colour Stripes
Image coloured purple	Image recoloured with a colour of your choice	Coloured quadrants applied to image	Image coloured with different coloured stripes

Commands

The **Commands** macros provide commonly-used commands, such as **Copy**, **Paste**, **Rotate**, and **Crop**. Use these to facilitate the basic functionality of PhotoPlus. For example, run the **Canvas Size** macro to adjust your canvas dimensions, or use **Flip Horizontal** to create a mirror image.

Original with selection area illustrated by ⌐⌐

Cut (selection)	Paste (as new layer)	Copy (selection)	Crop (selection)	Revert
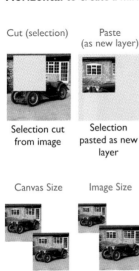				
Selection cut from image	Selection pasted as new layer	Selection area copied	Image cropped to size of selection	Image reverted to original

Canvas Size	Image Size	Flip Horizontal (layer)	Flip Vertical (layer)	Rotate 90 CW

Canvas cropped to specific size (250 x 350 pix)	Canvas resized to specific size (250 x 350 pix)	Layer flipped horizontally	Layer flipped vertically	Layer rotated 90° clockwise

Rotate 90 ACW	Rotate 180	Flatten Image	Fill	Clear
Layer rotated 90° anti-clockwise	Layer rotated 180°	All layers flattened into single layer	Selection filled with colour	Selection cleared

Effects

Use the **Effects** macros to quickly apply your favourite creative effects. PhotoPlus provides a range of effects, which you can use to produce subtle or dramatic results. Add a 'retro' feel to a portrait with **40's Glamour Model**. Soften and blur an image with **Dream**. For more extreme effects, try **Art** or **Shaken**.

Original with selection area illustrated by ⌐⌐, where applicable

Pencil Sketch	Pen Sketch	Art	Heavy Pencil Sketch
Image converted to pencil sketch	Image converted to pen sketch	Image reproduced as Pop Art	Image converted to heavy pencil sketch

Soft Pastel	40's Glamour Model	60's Sci-Fi	Negative
Image converted to soft pastel sketch	Black & white soft focus effect applied	Hue and Saturation values adjusted	Image converted into a negative

Vintage Photo	Wobble	Shaken	Dream
Sepia tint and soft focus applied	Wave distortion effect applied	Fragment blur applied	Diffuse glow applied

Disco

Neon effect applied
to image edges

Quick Sketch

Image converted
to quick sketch

Girl Pop

Filter effect
applied

Section Blur

Blur effect applied
to selected area

Night Vision

Lens distortion
effect applied

Multi Flares

Multi-coloured
lens flares applied

Amoeba

Image is
abstracted

Frames

The **Frames** macros allow you to frame your images with a single click.

Frame styles range from basic to classic and modern, all including a matte surround.

Original

Basic	Matte Surround	Frame and Surround	Wood Frame

Basic with options	Matte surround with options	Frame and surround with options	Wood Frame and Surround

Modern Frame	Metal Frame

Modern Frame and Surround	Metal Frame and Surround

Gradient Maps

You can use the **Gradient Fill Tool**, and the **Gradient** dialog settings to apply a predefined colour scheme to an image. You can also use the **Gradient Maps** macros to produce your favourite effects with a single command. Turn your colour photos into dramatic black and white images with the **Black and White** macro, or give an image an instant art effect with **Pop Art**.

Original

Black and White	Red	Pop Art	Summer
Colours are mapped to the basic Black to White Gradient Map	Colours are mapped to a Red to White Gradient Map	Colours are mapped to a Blue to Yellow to Red Gradient Map	Colours are mapped to a Red to Yellow to White Gradient Map

Black and White Mood	Hot Pink	Green	Blue
The image appears overexposed	Colours are mapped to a Red to Pink Gradient Map	Colours are mapped to a Green to White Gradient Map	Colours are mapped to a Blue to White Gradient Map

Yellow

Colours are
mapped to a
Yellow to White
Gradient Map

Orange

Colours are
mapped to an
Orange to White
Gradient Map

Purple

Colours are
mapped to a
Purple to White
Gradient Map

Pink

Colours are
mapped to a Pink
to White
Gradient Map

Rainbow

Colours are
mapped to a
multi-coloured
Gradient Map

Layout Blurs

Use the **Layout Blurs** macros to apply a range of blur effects to your images. For example, you can blur the edges of an image, while keeping the centre in focus; blur just the upper or lower portions of an image; or even 'frame' a photo with a larger, blurred version of the same image.

Original

Centred Small Image Big Blur

Centred Small Image Big B+W Blur

Centred Image Blur Surround

Centred Image B+W Blur Surround

Right Section Blur

Left Section Blur

Top Section Blur

Bottom Section Blur

Photography

Use the **Photography** macros to apply a range of photographic effects to your images. For example, you can change the exposure settings, sharpen an image, reduce saturation, or adjust brightness and contrast.

Original

Overexposed	Underexposed	Sharpen	Reduce Saturation	Quick Brightness & Contrast

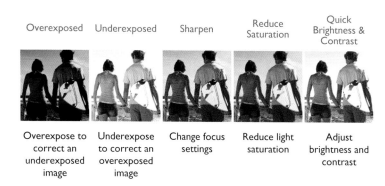

Overexpose to correct an underexposed image	Underexpose to correct an overexposed image	Change focus settings	Reduce light saturation	Adjust brightness and contrast

Remove Dust + Scratches

A quick fix for dusty or scratched photos! In the example below, we have restored a damaged image with the help of this macro.

Before   After

Selection

Grow Selection
Expands a selected area of an image to include all adjacent areas with the same colour value.

Find Similar
Identifies and selects all areas of an image that have the same colour value as the selected area.

Contract by 1 pixel
Reduces the size of a selected area by one pixel around its border.

Expand by 1 pixel
Increases the size of a selected area by one pixel around its border.

Border
Creates a second selection around the original selected area, forming a 'selection border.'

Feather
Crops a selected area and softens its border.

Feather and Centre
Crops a selected area, centres it, and softens its border.

Centre
Crops a selected area and centres it.

Centre – Shadow
Crops a selected area, centres it, and adds a shadow around its border.

Text Effects

Use the **Text Effects** macros to apply a range of creative effects to the text in your images.

Original

Spray Paint

Underwater

Water's Edge

Fuzz

Metal

Cut Out

Text Outlines

Use the **Text Outlines** macros to apply a range of outline effects to your text.

Textures

The **Textures** macros allow you to add a variety of texture effects to your images.

You can apply a simple **Wood** or **Stone** texture, or see your photos 'reproduced' on **Canvas** or **Recycled Paper**. Enable the dialogs and experiment with the various settings to produce some interesting results.

Original

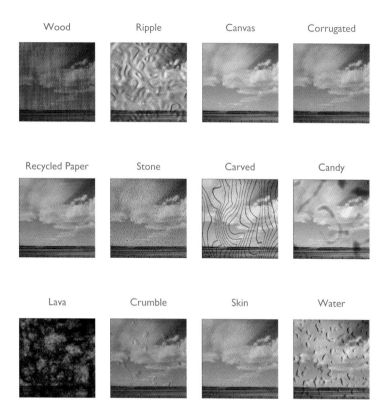

Wood

Ripple

Canvas

Corrugated

Recycled Paper

Stone

Carved

Candy

Lava

Crumble

Skin

Water

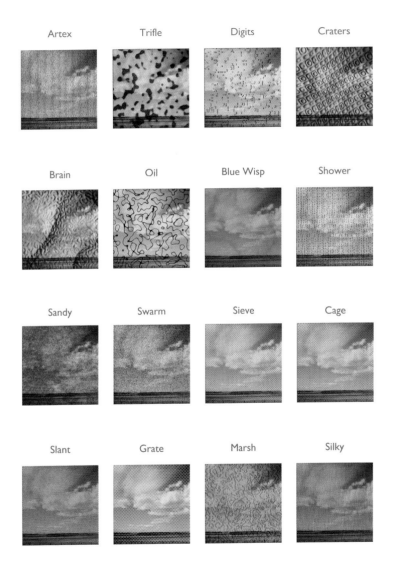

Artex	Trifle	Digits	Craters

Brain	Oil	Blue Wisp	Shower

Sandy	Swarm	Sieve	Cage

Slant	Grate	Marsh	Silky

Vignettes

Use the **Vignettes** macros to apply a range of surrounds. Apply a simple softened surround with **Oval Blur**, or add and adjust filter effects by choosing **Oval Blur w/options**.

Original

Oval Blur

Oval Large Blur

Customize your own **Oval Blur** effect in the **Filter Gallery** dialog. In this instance, we applied a **Pixelate** effect from the **Stylistic** category of the **Filter Gallery**.

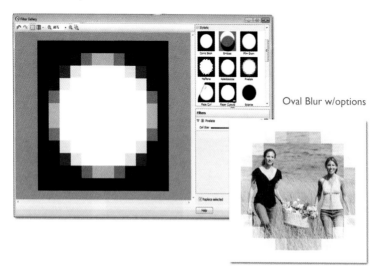

Oval Blur w/options

Square Blur

Square Large Blur

Customize your own **Square Blur** effect in the **Filter Gallery** dialog. In this instance, we applied a **Halftone** effect from the **Stylistic** category of the **Filter Gallery**.

Square Blur w/options

Brushes

PhotoPlus provides a large collection of creative brush tips stored in **Basic**, **Calligraphic**, **Effects**, **Media** and **Stamps** categories.

PhotoPlus also lets you import and create **Picture brushes**, edit preset brushes, and even create your own custom brushes from scratch!

For more information, see the *Painting* and *Stamping and spraying pictures* topics in the PhotoPlus Help.

Choosing brush tips

Use the **Brush Tip** tab to choose and customize brush tips for the painting tools, define custom brushes, and import Paint Shop Pro 'picture tubes.'

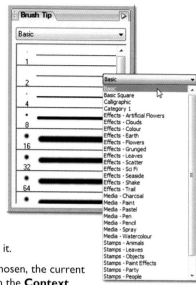

The tab displays a galleries of brushes grouped into various categories, accessible via the drop-down menu.

Each gallery sample shows the brush tip and stroke; the number indicates the brush diameter.

Simply click a brush tip to select it.

When any brush-based tool is chosen, the current brush is displayed as a sample on the **Context toolbar** and in the **Brush Options** dialog (discussed below).

Adjusting brushes

Once you have selected a brush tip, you can adjust its properties (opacity, size, flow, etc.) on the Context toolbar.

For more advanced options, click the **Brush** sample swatch to open the **Brush Options** dialog.

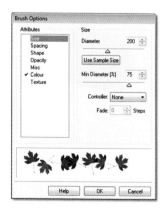

Saving brushes

After customizing a brush, you can save it as a gallery brush in a *user-created category*.

To add a new brush category and brush:

1   In the upper right corner of the **Brush Tip** tab, click the **Brush Tip Tab Menu** arrow button, and then click **Add Category**.

2   Name your category and click **OK**.

Your new category displays automatically in the drop-down list at the top of the **Brush Tip** tab.

3   Right-click in the gallery and click **New Brush**.

4   Name your brush and click **OK**. Your new brush is added to your custom category.

Editing brushes

Changes you make to the current brush via the **Brush** sample on the the Context toolbar only affect the current brush.

Brushes in the **Brush Tip** tab galleries are stored separately.

To change a gallery brush:

1   Add the brush to your own custom category (as described above).

2   Right-click the brush sample and choose **Brush Options**.

3   Use the **Brush Options** dialog to alter the properties of the brush.

To define a custom brush using a shape or a portion of an image:

1   Select the portion of your image that you want to use for your brush.

2   On the **Brush Tip** tab, choose one of your own user-created categories, then right-click in the gallery and choose **Define Brush**.

Brush tips

Basic
Round01
(1 pixel dia.)

Basic
Round02
(2 pixels dia.)

Basic
Round03
(4 pixels dia.)

Basic
Round04
(8 pixels dia.)

Basic
Round05
(16 pixels dia.)

Basic
Round06
(32 pixels dia.)

Basic
Round07
(64 pixels dia.)

Basic
Round08
(128 pixels dia.)

Basic
Round09
(256 pixels dia.)

Basic
Round Hard01
(1 pixels dia.)

Basic
Round Hard02
(2 pixels dia.)

Basic
Round Hard03
(4 pixels dia.)

Basic
Round Hard04
(8 pixels dia.)

Basic
Round Hard05
(16 pixels dia.)

Basic
Round Hard06
(32 pixels dia.)

Basic
Round Hard07
(64 pixels dia.)

Basic
Round Hard08
(128 pixels dia.)

Basic
Round Hard09
(256 pixels dia.)

Basic Square
Square01
(1 pixels dia.)

Basic Square
Square02
(2 pixels dia.)

Basic Square
Square03
(4 pixels dia.)

Basic Square
Square04
(8 pixels dia.)

Basic Square
Square05
(16 pixels dia.)

Basic Square
Square06
(32 pixels dia.)

Basic Square
Square07
(64 pixels dia.)

Basic Square
Square08
(128 pixels dia.)

Basic Square
Square09
(256 pixels dia.)

Basic Square
Square Hard01
(1 pixels dia.)

Basic Square
Square Hard02
(2 pixels dia.)

Basic Square
Square Hard03
(4 pixels dia.)

Basic Square
Square Hard04
(8 pixels dia.)

Basic Square
Square Hard05
(16 pixels dia.)

Basic Square
Square Hard06
(32 pixels dia.)

Basic Square
Square Hard07
(64 pixels dia.)

Basic Square
Square Hard08
(128 pixels dia.)

Basic Square
Square Hard09
(256 pixels dia.)

Calligraphic
Calligraphic Soft01
(10 pixels dia.)

Calligraphic
Calligraphic Soft02
(25 pixels dia.)

Calligraphic
Calligraphic Soft03
(50 pixels dia.)

Calligraphic
Calligraphic Soft04
(100 pixels dia.)

Calligraphic
Calligraphic Soft05
(200 pixels dia.)

Calligraphic
Calligraphic Hard01
(128 pixels dia.)

Calligraphic
Calligraphic Hard02
(25 pixels dia.)

Calligraphic
Calligraphic Hard03
(50 pixels dia.)

Calligraphic
Calligraphic Hard04
(100 pixels dia.)

Calligraphic

Calligraphic Hard05

(200 pixels dia.)

Calligraphic

Calligraphic Rounded Hard01

(10 pixels dia.)

Calligraphic

Calligraphic Rounded Hard02

(25 pixels dia.)

Calligraphic

Calligraphic Rounded Hard03

(50 pixels dia.)

Calligraphic

Calligraphic Rounded Hard04

(100 pixels dia.)

Calligraphic

Calligraphic Rounded Hard05

(200 pixels dia.)

Calligraphic

Calligraphic Hard Left01

(10 pixels dia.)

Calligraphic

Calligraphic Hard Left02

(25 pixels dia.)

Calligraphic

Calligraphic Hard Left03

(50 pixels dia.)

Calligraphic

Calligraphic Hard Left04

(100 pixels dia.)

Calligraphic

Calligraphic Hard Left05

(200 pixels dia.)

Effects - Artificial Flowers

Rose 01

(200 pixels dia.)

Effects - Artificial Flowers

Rose 02

(200 pixels dia.)

Effects - Artificial Flowers

Rose 03

(200 pixels dia.)

Effects - Artificial Flowers

Rose 04

(200 pixels dia.)

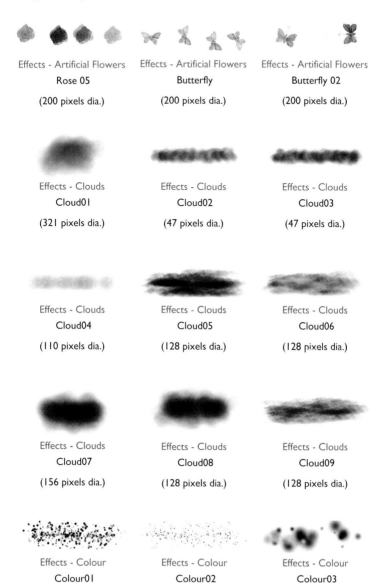

Effects - Artificial Flowers
Rose 05
(200 pixels dia.)

Effects - Artificial Flowers
Butterfly
(200 pixels dia.)

Effects - Artificial Flowers
Butterfly 02
(200 pixels dia.)

Effects - Clouds
Cloud01
(321 pixels dia.)

Effects - Clouds
Cloud02
(47 pixels dia.)

Effects - Clouds
Cloud03
(47 pixels dia.)

Effects - Clouds
Cloud04
(110 pixels dia.)

Effects - Clouds
Cloud05
(128 pixels dia.)

Effects - Clouds
Cloud06
(128 pixels dia.)

Effects - Clouds
Cloud07
(156 pixels dia.)

Effects - Clouds
Cloud08
(128 pixels dia.)

Effects - Clouds
Cloud09
(128 pixels dia.)

Effects - Colour
Colour01
(10 pixels dia.)

Effects - Colour
Colour02
(10 pixels dia.)

Effects - Colour
Colour03
(100 pixels dia.)

Effects - Colour
Colour04

(100 pixels dia.)

Effects - Colour
Colour05

(200 pixels dia.)

Effects - Colour
Colour06

(200 pixels dia.)

Effects - Colour
Colour07

(25 pixels dia.)

Effects - Colour
Colour08

(25 pixels dia.)

Effects - Colour
Colour09

(50 pixels dia.)

Effects - Colour
Colour10

(50 pixels dia.)

Effects - Colour
Colour11

(50 pixels dia.)

Effects - Earth
Blade of Grass01

(128 pixels dia.)

Effects - Earth
Blade of Grass02

(128 pixels dia.)

Effects - Earth
Blade of Grass03

(128 pixels dia.)

Effects - Earth
Blade of Grass04

(128 pixels dia.)

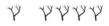

Effects - Earth
Branch01

(128 pixels dia.)

Effects - Earth
Branch02

(128 pixels dia.)

Effects - Earth
Leaf01

(128 pixels dia.)

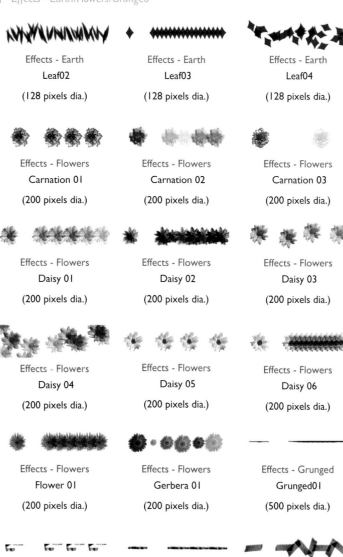

Effects - Earth
Leaf02
(128 pixels dia.)

Effects - Earth
Leaf03
(128 pixels dia.)

Effects - Earth
Leaf04
(128 pixels dia.)

Effects - Flowers
Carnation 01
(200 pixels dia.)

Effects - Flowers
Carnation 02
(200 pixels dia.)

Effects - Flowers
Carnation 03
(200 pixels dia.)

Effects - Flowers
Daisy 01
(200 pixels dia.)

Effects - Flowers
Daisy 02
(200 pixels dia.)

Effects - Flowers
Daisy 03
(200 pixels dia.)

Effects - Flowers
Daisy 04
(200 pixels dia.)

Effects - Flowers
Daisy 05
(200 pixels dia.)

Effects - Flowers
Daisy 06
(200 pixels dia.)

Effects - Flowers
Flower 01
(200 pixels dia.)

Effects - Flowers
Gerbera 01
(200 pixels dia.)

Effects - Grunged
Grunged01
(500 pixels dia.)

Effects - Grunged
Grunged02
(500 pixels dia.)

Effects - Grunged
Grunged03
(449 pixels dia.)

Effects - Grunged
Tape01
(400 pixels dia.)

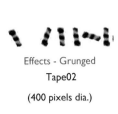

Effects - Grunged
Tape02
(400 pixels dia.)

Effects - Grunged
Crumple
(500 pixels dia.)

Effects - Grunged
Crumple Fade
(500 pixels dia.)

Effects - Grunged
Corner Crumple
(500 pixels dia.)

Effects - Grunged
Crease
(500 pixels dia.)

Effects - Grunged
Creased Line
(496 pixels dia.)

Effects - Grunged
Dots
(500 pixels dia.)

Effects - Grunged
Blot01
(150 pixels dia.)

Effects - Grunged
Blot02
(200 pixels dia.)

Effects - Grunged
Blot03
(200 pixels dia.)

Effects - Grunged
Blot04
(150 pixels dia.)

Effects - Grunged
Blot05
(200 pixels dia.)

Effects - Grunged
Blot06
(200 pixels dia.)

Effects - Grunged
Blot07
(200 pixels dia.)

Effects - Grunged
Blot08
(50 pixels dia.)

Effects - Grunged
Blot09
(150 pixels dia.)

Effects - Grunged
Blot10
(200 pixels dia.)

Effects - Grunged
Blot11
(200 pixels dia.)

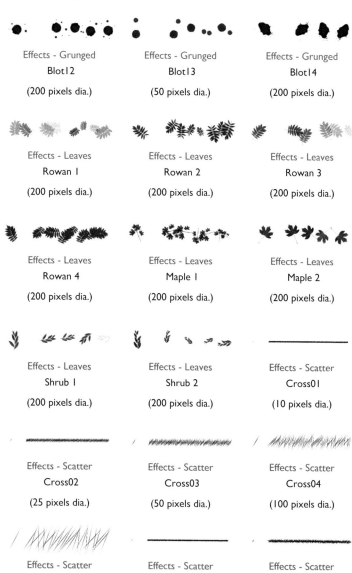

Effects - Grunged
Blot12

(200 pixels dia.)

Effects - Grunged
Blot13

(50 pixels dia.)

Effects - Grunged
Blot14

(200 pixels dia.)

Effects - Leaves
Rowan 1

(200 pixels dia.)

Effects - Leaves
Rowan 2

(200 pixels dia.)

Effects - Leaves
Rowan 3

(200 pixels dia.)

Effects - Leaves
Rowan 4

(200 pixels dia.)

Effects - Leaves
Maple 1

(200 pixels dia.)

Effects - Leaves
Maple 2

(200 pixels dia.)

Effects - Leaves
Shrub 1

(200 pixels dia.)

Effects - Leaves
Shrub 2

(200 pixels dia.)

Effects - Scatter
Cross01

(10 pixels dia.)

Effects - Scatter
Cross02

(25 pixels dia.)

Effects - Scatter
Cross03

(50 pixels dia.)

Effects - Scatter
Cross04

(100 pixels dia.)

Effects - Scatter
Cross05

(200 pixels dia.)

Effects - Scatter
Straws01

(10 pixels dia.)

Effects - Scatter
Straws02

(25 pixels dia.)

Effects - Scatter
Straws03
(50 pixels dia.)

Effects - Scatter
Straws04
(100 pixels dia.)

Effects - Scatter
Straws05
(200 pixels dia.)

Effects - Scatter
Wild01
(10 pixels dia.)

Effects - Scatter
Wild02
(25 pixels dia.)

Effects - Scatter
Wild03
(50 pixels dia.)

Effects - Scatter
Wild04
(100 pixels dia.)

Effects - Scatter
Wild05
(200 pixels dia.)

Effects - Scatter
Wild Scatter01
(10 pixels dia.)

Effects - Scatter
Wild Scatter02
(25 pixels dia.)

Effects - Scatter
Wild Scatter03
(50 pixels dia.)

Effects - Scatter
Wild Scatter04
(100 pixels dia.)

Effects - Scatter
Wild Scatter05
(200 pixels dia.)

Effects - Sci-Fi
Sci-fi 01
(197 pixels dia.)

Effects - Sci-Fi
Sci-fi 02
(85 pixels dia.)

Effects - Sci-Fi
Sci-fi 03
(150 pixels dia.)

Effects - Sci-Fi
Sci-fi 04
(280 pixels dia.)

Effects - Sci-Fi
Sci-fi 05
(99 pixels dia.)

Effects - Sci-Fi
Sci-fi 06
(82 pixels dia.)

Effects - Sci-Fi
Sci-fi 07
(177 pixels dia.)

Effects - Sci-Fi
Sci-fi 08
(251 pixels dia.)

Effects - Sci-Fi
Sci-fi 09
(106 pixels dia.)

Effects - Seaside
Shell 1
(200 pixels dia.)

Effects - Seaside
Shell 1 Inside
(200 pixels dia.)

Effects - Seaside
Shell 2
(200 pixels dia.)

Effects - Seaside
Shell 2 Inside
(200 pixels dia.)

Effects - Seaside
Shell 3
(200 pixels dia.)

Effects - Seaside
Shell 3 Inside
(200 pixels dia.)

Effects - Seaside
Shell 4
(200 pixels dia.)

Effects - Seaside
Shell 4 Inside
(200 pixels dia.)

Effects - Seaside
Shell 5
(200 pixels dia.)

Effects - Seaside
Shell 5 Inside
(200 pixels dia.)

Effects - Seaside
Sea Urchin
(200 pixels dia.)

Effects - Seaside
Sea Urchin Inside
(200 pixels dia.)

Effects - Shake
Shake01
(128 pixels dia.)

Effects - Shake
Shake02
(128 pixels dia.)

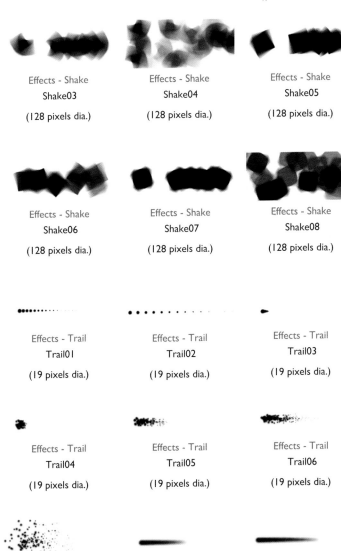

Effects - Shake
Shake03
(128 pixels dia.)

Effects - Shake
Shake04
(128 pixels dia.)

Effects - Shake
Shake05
(128 pixels dia.)

Effects - Shake
Shake06
(128 pixels dia.)

Effects - Shake
Shake07
(128 pixels dia.)

Effects - Shake
Shake08
(128 pixels dia.)

Effects - Trail
Trail01
(19 pixels dia.)

Effects - Trail
Trail02
(19 pixels dia.)

Effects - Trail
Trail03
(19 pixels dia.)

Effects - Trail
Trail04
(19 pixels dia.)

Effects - Trail
Trail05
(19 pixels dia.)

Effects - Trail
Trail06
(19 pixels dia.)

Effects - Trail
Trail07
(19 pixels dia.)

Effects - Trail
Trail08
(32 pixels dia.)

Effects - Trail
Trail09
(32 pixels dia.)

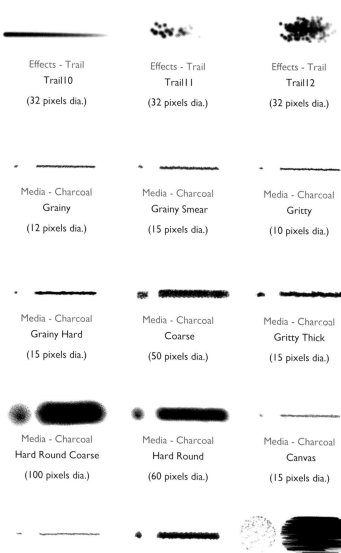

Effects - Trail
Trail10
(32 pixels dia.)

Effects - Trail
Trail11
(32 pixels dia.)

Effects - Trail
Trail12
(32 pixels dia.)

Media - Charcoal
Grainy
(12 pixels dia.)

Media - Charcoal
Grainy Smear
(15 pixels dia.)

Media - Charcoal
Gritty
(10 pixels dia.)

Media - Charcoal
Grainy Hard
(15 pixels dia.)

Media - Charcoal
Coarse
(50 pixels dia.)

Media - Charcoal
Gritty Thick
(15 pixels dia.)

Media - Charcoal
Hard Round Coarse
(100 pixels dia.)

Media - Charcoal
Hard Round
(60 pixels dia.)

Media - Charcoal
Canvas
(15 pixels dia.)

Media - Charcoal
Coarse Soft
(10 pixels dia.)

Media - Charcoal
Rough
(30 pixels dia.)

Media - Paint
Acrylic Round Hard
(120 pixels dia.)

Media - Paint
Acrylic Round Smear

(150 pixels dia.)

Media - Paint
Acrylic Round

(120 pixels dia.)

Media - Paint
Acrylic Flat Hard

(250 pixels dia.)

Media - Paint
Acrylic Flat Soft

(250 pixels dia.)

Media - Paint
Acrylic Flat Hard

(251 pixels dia.)

Media - Paint
Acrylic Flat Soft

(254 pixels dia.)

Media - Paint
Acrylic Chiselled Hard

(250 pixels dia.)

Media - Paint
Acrylic Chiselled Soft

(250 pixels dia.)

Media - Paint
Round

(150 pixels dia.)

Media - Paint
Splodgy

(100 pixels dia.)

Media - Paint
Grainy

(150 pixels dia.)

Media - Paint
Grainy Heavy

(150 pixels dia.)

Media - Pen
Standard Pen

(15 pixels dia.)

Media - Pen
Marker Pen

(70 pixels dia.)

Media - Pen
Random Hatch Marks

(64 pixels dia.)

Media - Pen
Felt Tip Thin

(8pixels dia.)

Media - Pen
Felt Tip Thick

(20 pixels dia.)

Media - Pencil
Standard
(5 pixels dia.)

Media - Pencil
Diagonal Scribble
(128 pixels dia.)

Media - Pencil
Scribble
(128 pixels dia.)

Media - Pencil
Random Scribble
(128 pixels dia.)

Media - Pencil
Coarse
(8 pixels dia.)

Media - Pencil
Hatch Marks
(128 pixels dia.)

Media - Pencil
Random Hatch Marks
(128 pixels dia.)

Media - Pencil
Thick Light
(28 pixels dia.)

Media - Pencil
Thick Heavy
(24 pixels dia.)

Media - Spray
Horizontal X-Small
(10 pixels dia.)

Media - Spray
Horizontal Small
(25 pixels dia.)

Media - Spray
Horizontal Medium
(50 pixels dia.)

Media - Spray
Horizontal Large
(100 pixels dia.)

Media - Spray
Horizontal X-Large
(200 pixels dia.)

Media - Spray
Scatter X-Small
(10 pixels dia.)

Media - Spray
Scatter Small
(25 pixels dia.)

Media - Spray
Scatter Medium
(50 pixels dia.)

Media - Spray
Scatter Large
(100 pixels dia.)

Media - Spray
Scatter X-Large

(200 pixels dia.)

Media - Spray
Scatter Soft X-Small

(10 pixels dia.)

Media - Spray
Scatter Soft Small

(25 pixels dia.)

Media - Spray
Scatter Soft Medium

(50 pixels dia.)

Media - Spray
Scatter Soft Large

(100 pixels dia.)

Media - Spray
Scatter Soft X-Large

(200 pixels dia.)

Media - Spray
Sponge X-Small

(10 pixels dia.)

Media - Spray
Sponge Small

(25 pixels dia.)

Media - Spray
Sponge Medium

(50 pixels dia.)

Media - Spray
Sponge Large

(100 pixels dia.)

Media - Spray
Sponge X-Large

(200 pixels dia.)

Media - Spray
Tight X-Small

(10 pixels dia.)

Media - Spray
Tight Small

(25 pixels dia.)

Media - Spray
Tight Medium

(50 pixels dia.)

Media - Spray
Tight Large

(100 pixels dia.)

Media - Spray
Tight X-Large

(200 pixels dia.)

Media - Spray
Vertical X-Small

(10 pixels dia.)

Media - Spray
Vertical Small

(25 pixels dia.)

Media - Spray

Vertical Medium

(50 pixels dia.)

Media - Spray

Vertical Large

(100 pixels dia.)

Media - Spray

Vertical X-Large

(200 pixels dia.)

Media - Watercolour

Round Heavy

(230 pixels dia.)

Media - Watercolour

Round Light

(230 pixels dia.)

Media - Watercolour

Coarse

(100 pixels dia.)

Media - Watercolour

Round Wet

(230 pixels dia.)

Media - Watercolour

Coarse Heavy

(230 pixels dia.)

Media - Watercolour

Coarse Smudgy

(150 pixels dia.)

Media - Watercolour

Coarse Wet

(200 pixels dia.)

Media - Watercolour

Bristle Wet

(220 pixels dia.)

Media - Watercolour

Bristle

(220 pixels dia.)

Media - Watercolour

Bristle Smudgy

(250 pixels dia.)

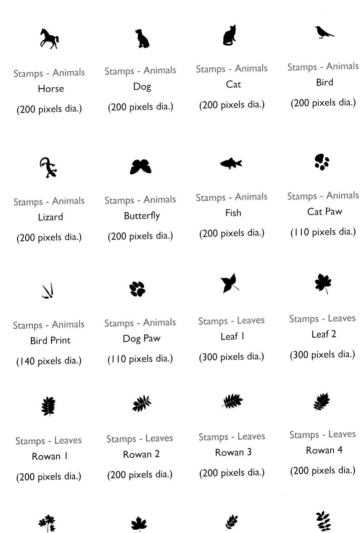

Stamps - Animals
Horse
(200 pixels dia.)

Stamps - Animals
Dog
(200 pixels dia.)

Stamps - Animals
Cat
(200 pixels dia.)

Stamps - Animals
Bird
(200 pixels dia.)

Stamps - Animals
Lizard
(200 pixels dia.)

Stamps - Animals
Butterfly
(200 pixels dia.)

Stamps - Animals
Fish
(200 pixels dia.)

Stamps - Animals
Cat Paw
(110 pixels dia.)

Stamps - Animals
Bird Print
(140 pixels dia.)

Stamps - Animals
Dog Paw
(110 pixels dia.)

Stamps - Leaves
Leaf 1
(300 pixels dia.)

Stamps - Leaves
Leaf 2
(300 pixels dia.)

Stamps - Leaves
Rowan 1
(200 pixels dia.)

Stamps - Leaves
Rowan 2
(200 pixels dia.)

Stamps - Leaves
Rowan 3
(200 pixels dia.)

Stamps - Leaves
Rowan 4
(200 pixels dia.)

Stamps - Leaves
Maple 1
(200 pixels dia.)

Stamps - Leaves
Maple 2
(200 pixels dia.)

Stamps - Leaves
Ash 1
(200 pixels dia.)

Stamps - Leaves
Ash 2
(200 pixels dia.)

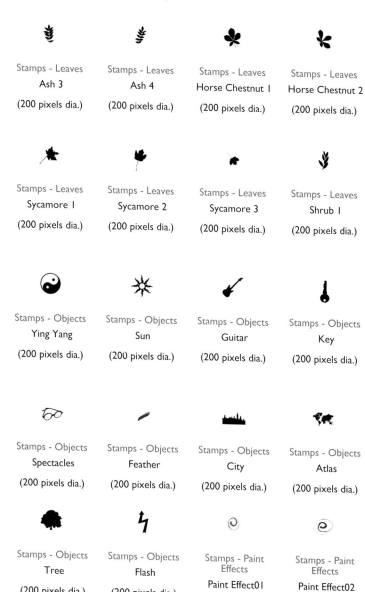

Stamps - Leaves
Ash 3
(200 pixels dia.)

Stamps - Leaves
Ash 4
(200 pixels dia.)

Stamps - Leaves
Horse Chestnut 1
(200 pixels dia.)

Stamps - Leaves
Horse Chestnut 2
(200 pixels dia.)

Stamps - Leaves
Sycamore 1
(200 pixels dia.)

Stamps - Leaves
Sycamore 2
(200 pixels dia.)

Stamps - Leaves
Sycamore 3
(200 pixels dia.)

Stamps - Leaves
Shrub 1
(200 pixels dia.)

Stamps - Objects
Ying Yang
(200 pixels dia.)

Stamps - Objects
Sun
(200 pixels dia.)

Stamps - Objects
Guitar
(200 pixels dia.)

Stamps - Objects
Key
(200 pixels dia.)

Stamps - Objects
Spectacles
(200 pixels dia.)

Stamps - Objects
Feather
(200 pixels dia.)

Stamps - Objects
City
(200 pixels dia.)

Stamps - Objects
Atlas
(200 pixels dia.)

Stamps - Objects
Tree
(200 pixels dia.)

Stamps - Objects
Flash
(200 pixels dia.)

Stamps - Paint Effects
Paint Effect01
(200 pixels dia.)

Stamps - Paint Effects
Paint Effect02
(200 pixels dia.)

Stamps - Paint
Effects
Paint Effect03

(200 pixels dia.)

Stamps - Paint
Effects
Paint Effect04

(200 pixels dia.)

Stamps - Paint
Effects
Paint Effect05

(200 pixels dia.)

Stamps - Paint
Effects
Paint Effect06

(200 pixels dia.)

Stamps - Paint
Effects
Paint Effect07

(150 pixels dia.)

Stamps - Paint
Effects
Paint Effect08

(150 pixels dia.)

Stamps - Paint
Effects
Paint Effect09

(200 pixels dia.)

Stamps - Paint
Effects
Paint Effect10

(200 pixels dia.)

Stamps - Paint
Effects
Paint Effect11

(200 pixels dia.)

Stamps - Paint
Effects
Paint Effect12

(200 pixels dia.)

Stamps - Party
Party01

(67 pixels dia.)

Stamps - Party
Party02

(78 pixels dia.)

Stamps - Party
Party03

(157 pixels dia.)

Stamps - Party
Party04

(60 pixels dia.)

Stamps - Party
Party05

(96 pixels dia.)

Stamps - Party
Party06

(50 pixels dia.)

Stamps - Party
Party07

(51 pixels dia.)

Stamps - Party
Party08

(8 pixels dia.)

Stamps - Party
Party09

(157 pixels dia.)

Stamps - People
Eye

(100 pixels dia.)

Stamps - People
Female Face

(250 pixels dia.)

Stamps - People
Male Face

(200 pixels dia.)

Stamps - People
Jogging

(200 pixels dia.)

Stamps - People
Footballer

(200 pixels dia.)

Stamps - People
Rambler

(200 pixels dia.)

Stamps - People
Lips

(200 pixels dia.)

Stamps - People
Business Woman

(200 pixels dia.)

Stamps - People
Business Man

(200 pixels dia.)

Stamps - People
Hand

(200 pixels dia.)

Stamps - People
Crowd

(200 pixels dia.)

Stamps - Seaside
Shell I

(200 pixels dia.)

Stamps - Seaside
Shell 2

(200 pixels dia.)

Stamps - Seaside
Shell 3

(200 pixels dia.)

Stamps - Seaside
Shell 4

(200 pixels dia.)

Stamps - Seaside
Shell 5

(200 pixels dia.)

Stamps - Seaside
Sea Urchin

(200 pixels dia.)

Stamps - Shapes
Stamp01

(151 pixels dia.)

Stamps - Shapes
Stamp02

(108 pixels dia.)

Stamps - Shapes
Stamp03

(82 pixels dia.)

Stamps - Shapes
Stamp04

(82 pixels dia.)

Stamps - Shapes
Stamp05

(82 pixels dia.)

Stamps - Shapes
Stamp06

(151 pixels dia.)

Stamps - Splats
Splat Stamp 01

(200 pixels dia.)

Stamps - Splats
Splat Stamp 02

(150 pixels dia.)

Stamps - Splats
Splat Stamp 03

(150 pixels dia.)

Stamps - Splats
Splat Stamp 04

(150 pixels dia.)

Stamps - Splats
Splat Stamp 05

(300 pixels dia.)

Stamps - Transport
Motorbike

(200 pixels dia.)

Stamps - Transport
Car

(200 pixels dia.)

Stamps - Transport
Bicycle

(200 pixels dia.)

Stamps - Transport
Tram

(200 pixels dia.)

Stamps - Transport
Airship

(200 pixels dia.)

Stamps - Transport
Aeroplane01

(200 pixels dia.)

Stamps - Transport
Aeroplane02

(200 pixels dia.)

Stamps - Transport
Sailboat

(200 pixels dia.)

Stamps - Transport
Helicopter

(200 pixels dia.)

Stamps - Transport
Scooter

Stamps - Vector
Branch 01

Stamps - Vector
Branch 02

Stamps - Vector
Branch 03

Stamps - Vector
Branch 04

Stamps - Vector
Branch 05

Stamps - Vector
Branch 06

Stamps - Vector
Branch 07

Stamps - Vector
Decorative 01

Stamps - Vector
Decorative 02

Stamps - Vector
Floral 01

Stamps - Vector
Floral 02

Stamps - Vector
Floral 03

Stamps - Vector
Floral 04

Stamps - Vector
Floral 05

Stamps - Vector
Scatter 01

Stamps - Vector
Scatter 02

Stamps - Vector
Scatter 03

Stamps - Vector
Scatter 04

Stamps - Vector
Twirl 01

Stamps - Vector
Twirl 02

Stamps - Wires
Wires01

Stamps - Wires
Wires02

Stamps - Wires
Wires03

Stamps - Wires
Wires04

Picture brushes

Confetti
Confetti Circles

Confetti
Confetti Hearts

Confetti
Confetti Horseshoe

Confetti
Confetti Squares

Confetti
Confetti Stars

Simple
Blue Tube

Simple
Coloured Tube

Simple
Gold Tube

Simple
Green Tube

Simple
Luminous Tube

Simple
Magenta Tube

Simple
Orange Tube

Simple
Purple Tube

Simple
Red Tube

Simple
Sea Green Tube

Simple
Silver Tube

Spirals and Stars
Blue Corkscrew

Spirals and Stars
Blue Stars

Spirals and Stars
Green Corkscrew

Spirals and Stars
Multi Swirls

Spirals and Stars
Red Burn Stars

Spirals and Stars
Red Corkscrew

Spirals and Stars
Red Multi Stars

Spirals and Stars
Shiny Spirals

Spirals and Stars
Sparkle

Spirals and Stars
Steel Corkscrew

Spirals and Stars
Tropical Carpet

Splat
Arcade

Splat
Camouflage01

Splat
Camouflage02

Splat
Camouflage03

Splat
Camouflage04

Splat
Dots

Splat
Green Splot Tube

Splat
Gunge

Splat
Multi-spots

Splat
Purple Splot Tube

Splat
Red Splot Tube

PhotoFix Presets

New to PhotoPlus X4, **PhotoFix** provides an environment that simplifies the often complicated process of image correction.

A range of ready-made presets is also included in the **Favourites** tab!

For more information about **PhotoFix**, see *Using PhotoFix* in the PhotoPlus Help.

To launch **PhotoFix**, click 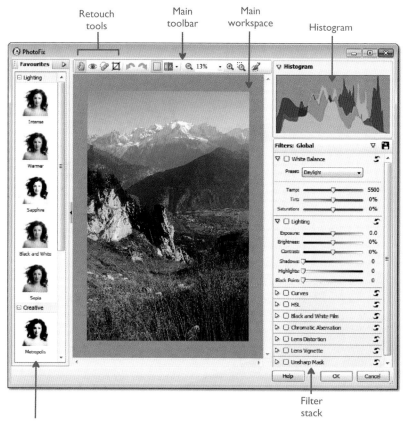 on the **Photo Studio** toolbar (or select it from the the **Effects** menu).

Retouch tools

Main toolbar

Main workspace

Histogram

Filter stack

Favourites Tab

PhotoFix stores preset and custom favourites together on the **Favourites** tab. This chapter showcases the preset filters provided.

For more information on adding and managing PhotoFix favourites, see the PhotoPlus Help.

Lighting

Intense

Original Image

Warmer

Original Image

Sapphire

Original Image

Black and White

Original Image

Sepia

Original Image

Creative

Metropolis

Original Image

Glamour

Original Image

Old Photo

Original Image

Etching

Original Image

Intense Sepia

Original Image